THE RIGHT TO PRIVACY

BY STEPHEN GOODE

D1745482

A GROLIER COMPANY

FRANKLIN WATTS
New York □ London □ Toronto
Sydney □ 1983

This book is
dedicated to

PORTIA HILL
McDONALD,
1910–1979

The Ablest
of Teachers

7/3/84

Library of Congress Cataloging in Publication Data

Goode, Stephen.
The right to privacy.

Bibliography: p.
Includes index.
Summary: Discusses the collection of information
about individuals by government agencies, law
enforcement officials, credit bureaus, insurance
companies, and other investigators, and the threat
to personal privacy represented by searches
and seizures, eavesdropping, personality tests,
polygraphs, and computer technology.
1. Privacy, Right of—United States—
Juvenile literature. [1. Privacy, Right of. 2. Civil rights]
    I. Title.

| KF1262.Z9G6 | 1983 | 342.73'0858 | 83-10649 |
| ISBN 0-531-04585-4 | | 347.302858 | |

CONTENTS

We are rapidly entering the age of no privacy, where everyone is open to surveillance at all times; where there are no secrets from the Government. The aggressive breaches of privacy by the Government increase with geometric proportions. Wiretapping and "bugging" run rampant, without effective judicial or legislative control.

Secret observation booths in government offices and closed television circuits in industry, extending even to rest rooms, are common. Offices, conference rooms, hotel rooms and even bedrooms are "bugged" for the convenience of the Government. Personality tests seek to ferret out a man's innermost thoughts. . . . Federal agents are often "wired" so that their conversations are either recorded on their persons or transmitted to tape recorders some blocks away. . . . They have broken and entered homes to obtain evidence. . . . The dossiers on all citizens mount in number and increase in size. Now they are being put on computers so that by pressing one button all the miserable, the sick, the suspect, the unpopular, the off-beat people of the nation can be instantly identified. These examples and many others demonstrate an alarming trend whereby the privacy and dignity of our citizens is being whittled away by sometimes imperceptible steps. Taken individually, each step may be of little consequence. But when viewed as a whole, there begins to emerge a society quite unlike any we have seen — a society in which Government may intrude into the secret regions of a man's life at will.

From the dissent of
Justice William O. Douglas in the
case of *Osborn* v. *U.S.* (1966)

THE RIGHT TO PRIVACY

1
THE ASSAULT ON PRIVACY

There was of course no way of
knowing whether you were being
watched at any given moment.
How often, or on what system, the
Thought Police plugged in on any
individual wire was guesswork.
It was even conceivable that they
watched everybody all the time.
But at any rate they could plug in
your wire whenever they wanted
to. You had to live—did live, from
habit that had become instinct—in
the assumption that every sound
you made was overheard, and, except in darkness, every movement
scrutinized.

From George Orwell's *1984*

More than ever before, Americans are concerned about the right to privacy. In his best-selling book, *The Naked Society* (1964)—one of the first popular works to discuss the threat to privacy in modern America—Vance Packard warned that "the surveillance of citizens in the United States...has been growing year by year."

"Are there loose in our modern world forces that threaten to annihilate everybody's privacy?" Packard asked. "And if such forces are indeed loose," he went on, are they leading to conditions that "endanger the freedom of modern man?"

Packard answered "yes" to both questions. Privacy, he concluded, was under severe threat and, as the right to privacy diminished, he feared that the other freedoms enjoyed by Americans would likewise diminish and wither away.

Packard had touched upon an issue that bothered many Americans. Fifteen years later, that issue was still very much in evidence. In 1979, a Louis Harris poll questioned Americans about the right to privacy. The figures were startling.

Sixty-four percent of those polled declared that they had a "real concern" about the loss of personal privacy in recent years. Eighty-one percent believed that they had been unfairly penalized because private information about their lives remained too long in the data banks and computers of government agencies and private business.

Seventy-two percent thought that government and private-sector investigators asked for data that should remain strictly private. Seventy-six percent of those polled were in agreement with the statement that "Americans begin surrendering their privacy the day they open their first charge account, take out a loan, buy something on the installment plan, or apply for a credit card."

When asked if the right to privacy should be added to the list of the traditional rights enjoyed by American citizens—such as the rights to life, liberty, and the pursuit of happiness—those who were polled agreed by a margin of 76 to 17 percent that the right to privacy should be added to that list.

But more ominously, 34 percent felt that the United States was "very close" to a realization of the world imagined by George Orwell in his novel *1984*, a world where technological innovation and totalitarian government permit "Thought Police" to follow one's every move, at home or at work. Thirty-nine percent of the poll thought that we were "somewhat close" to the society of *1984*. Most Americans, pollster Louis Harris concluded, seem to believe that "we might arrive in 1984 right on time."*

WHY IS PRIVACY IN AMERICA ENDANGERED?

Vance Packard noted five reasons why privacy was under assault in American society: (1) the "bigness" of modern America, with its large government bureaucracy, its large corporations, and large population concentrated in enormous urban centers; (2) the threat to American security presented by cold-war tension and the rapidly growing crime rate since World War II; (3) American affluence; (4) the development of a sophisticated technology that has expanded the power of the human eye, ear, and memory; and (5) the existence of a large number of investigative services and agencies whose sole purpose is to collect and record data about American citizens. These factors are even truer today than they were when Packard wrote in 1964.

In order for the large federal bureaucracy to produce the many services it provides the American people, it must know intimate details about their lives. Social Security and welfare agencies must know income, health, and family status, among other things. The Internal Revenue Service must keep tabs on salaries, dividends, and other financial transactions.

---

*The poll was commissioned by the Sentry Insurance Company and was conducted with the assistance of Alan Westin, a highly regarded expert on privacy in the United States. The poll was published by Sentry Insurance, under the title "The Dimensions of Privacy."

Similarly, large corporations that hire many thousands of employees must maintain dossiers where data on employee pension plans, medical insurance, and personal abilities are recorded. As more than one author has observed, information and data are the "fuel" that keeps American society moving. Without a constant supply and flow of information, what efficiency and order that society has achieved would collapse—government could not supply benefits to millions of citizens; employers would be hard-pressed to take care of employees.

Federal, state, and local law enforcement officials tell us that law enforcement in the United States would be much less efficient if they did not have the power to investigate and collect data on individuals they regard as criminals or subversives. The FBI closely monitors the activities of members of organized crime and of radical political groups it believes threaten the "American way of life."

State and local police likewise keep track of the activities of criminals. Law enforcement investigations frequently intrude into the lives of innocent citizens as well as those of criminals. But, law enforcement officials tell us, this is the price we must pay if modern America is to be kept orderly and secure.

American affluence has contributed to the loss of privacy in a number of ways. Most buying today is done on credit. But to buy on credit, a consumer must agree to turn over information about his or her income, life-style, and other personal data to consumer bureaus. Consumer bureaus may also conduct their own investigations into the private lives of American citizens in order to determine if they are worthy recipients of credit.

Increased affluence has also meant an increased demand for insurance. Insurance companies, too, demand to know a great deal about the people they are asked to insure before granting a policy. This information, like that collected by credit bureaus, goes into permanent files that are constantly updated.

The collection of information by government agencies, by law enforcement officials, credit bureaus, and insurance companies has been made more sinister by the development of modern technology. In earlier times, the collection of information was relatively harmless. Collected data went into files that were cumbersome and where retrieval was slow and awkward.

Today, however, the computer has rendered all that obsolete. Data and information can be recalled almost instantly and be sent anywhere in the world in a matter of seconds. In addition, sophisticated eavesdropping devices make it possible to overhear and record conversations once regarded as private and confidential.

Finally, the demand for information in modern America has given birth to numerous agencies and businesses that do nothing but collect data and perform investigations. These agencies make use of modern technology. They perform investigations for credit bureaus, insurance companies, and for the government. Often, their work involves asking questions of friends and relatives of an individual under investigation, delving into his or her bank accounts and medical records, and other private background material.

THE IMPORTANCE
OF PRIVACY

Webster's New Collegiate Dictionary defines privacy as the "state of being apart from company or observation; also, secrecy." The right to privacy, then, would be the right to be free from company or observation; the right to seclusion and to have secrets. The late Supreme Court Associate Justice Louis Brandeis called the right to privacy "the right to be let alone."*

Privacy is important for a number of reasons. Psychologists and sociologists tell us that it is important for every individual to have a sense of autonomy, a feeling that there is an area of an individual's life that is totally under his or her control, an area that is free from outside intrusion.

---

*Brandeis borrowed the phrase "the right to be let alone" from Judge Thomas M. Cooley's *A Treatise on the Law of Torts* (1888). Cooley was an influential nineteenth century American jurist.

More than one hundred and fifty years ago, the English writer Maria Edgeworth noted that children want and need privacy. "Nothing hurts young people more," Edgeworth wrote in her *Essays on Practical Education* (1822), "than to be watched continually about their feelings, to have their sensibility measured by the surveying eye of the unmerciful spectator. Under the constraint of such examinations, they can think of nothing but that they are looked at, and feel nothing but shame or apprehension."

In an article entitled "Some Psychological Aspects of Privacy" in the Spring 1966 issue of *Law and Contemporary Problems*, the psychologist Sydney Jourard wrote that privacy "is experienced as 'room to grow in.'" Genuine privacy, he continued, is "freedom from interference" and the freedom "to explore" and "to pursue experimental projects in science, art, work, play, and living." Privacy, he added, is the "concomitant of freedom."

Without privacy, Jourard went on, an individual's health is endangered. "The experience of psychotherapists and students of personality growth," he explained, "has shown that people maintain themselves in physical health and in psychological and spiritual well-being when they have a 'private place,' some locus that is inviolable by others except at the person's express invitation."*

According to Jourard, this necessary "private place" or "locus" may be a physical location, such as a favorite room. It may also be a group of people "who share the ideals of the person in question." What is important about the private place is that it be a place where the individual

---

*The effects of a lack of privacy on emotional and physical health are vividly portrayed in Patricia Hearst's *Every Secret Thing* (1982). Ms. Hearst, a member of a wealthy and prominent newspaper family, was kidnapped in February 1974 by a band of leftist terrorists. In her book, Hearst describes how the terrorists kept her for almost sixty days in a small, dark closet. She had no privacy. Members of the band could enter the closet at will, shout at her and abuse her. At no time was she allowed to feel free of possible harassment and humiliation by her captors. She was reduced to a state of fear and trembling.

Even after release from the closet, Patricia Hearst was allowed no privacy. The terrorists kept close personal watch over her. As a result, her personality altered and health deteriorated. The once nonpolitical heir to a family fortune joined the terrorist band, convinced that she had no life apart from the band itself.

"can do or be as he likes and feels" and where "he does not need to fear external sanctions" or possible intrusion or manipulation from the outside.

The erosion of privacy in recent years, Jourard warned, will eventually mean a decrease in the general level of emotional and physical health, a weakened "commitment to society" on the part of American citizens, and possible "social stagnation" of American society.

PRIVACY AND DEMOCRACY

If privacy is important to the healthy growth and development of the individual, it is essential to democracy. Democracy stresses the worthiness of every individual and the importance of personal dignity. Without the right to privacy, there can be little human dignity or individuality.

The noted historian Clinton Rossiter pointed this out when he wrote that privacy "seeks to erect an unbreachable wall of dignity and reserve against the entire world." Furthermore, Rossiter believed that "the free man is the private man, the man who still keeps some of his thoughts and judgments entirely to himself, who feels no over-riding compulsion to share everything of value with others, not even those he loves and trusts. Privacy," he concluded, "is a special kind of independence, which can be understood as an attempt to secure autonomy in at least a few personal and spiritual concerns, if necessary in defiance of all the pressures of modern society."

Rossiter and other close observers of American society hold that the connection between democracy and privacy is so intimate that one cannot exist without the other. To be free, they point out, individuals must have control of their own lives and private matters; they must regard themselves as the "masters of their own fate."

One of the best discussions of the relationship between privacy and democracy appeared in Edward Shils's *The Torment of Secrecy* (1956). Shils, one of America's foremost sociologists, regarded privacy and autonomy as a "first principle" of democracy. Privacy and autonomy, Shils wrote, involve "the right to make decisions, to promulgate rules of action, to dispose over resources and to recruit associates in accordance with criteria which the individual... deems appropriate."

Privacy and autonomy, he went on, also assume that "by and large, an individual's... life is" his or her "own business" and that "only exceptional circumstances justify enforced and entire disclosure, to the eyes of the broader public" of the individual's private affairs. "If most men, most of the time, regarded themselves as their brother-citizens' keeper," Shils concluded, then "freedom, which flourishes in the indifference of privacy, would be abolished."

The goal of a democratic society, he added, should be to achieve a state of civility. A state of civility, Shils explained, was one in which enough personal privacy existed to allow and stimulate personal creativity. But at the same time, sufficient publicity about current affairs was to be allowed so that the public could arrive at informed conclusions.

PRIVACY AND TOTALITARIANISM

One way to appreciate the importance of privacy in a democracy is to look at what happens to privacy under totalitarian governments. Totalitarian governments permit as little personal privacy as possible. They look upon privacy as "decadent" and "antisocial" and stress the importance, not of individuality, but of a person's total loyalty to the goals of the state.

Nazi Germany between 1933 and 1945 was a totalitarian state. Privacy in Nazi Germany, noted Senator Edward Long (Democrat, Missouri), in his book *The Intruders* (1966), was almost nonexistent. "Electronic eavesdropping and telephone wire taps," he wrote, "were so commonplace that Germans came to assume that anything they said could be overheard by secret police."

The secret police also used other means to intrude upon privacy. A sudden knock on the door in the middle of the night, Long claimed, would be followed by the "invasion of the home, and the dragging or driving of people in their night clothes into the streets." Even when an individual was not under investigation or surveillance, Long continued, "he was always possessed by the fear that he might be. Along with this was the fear that the secret police might descend on him at any time."

What this "brutal invasion of privacy" was designed to accomplish, Senator Long explained, was "the maximum in intimidation and fear. Destruction of the individual's sense of his own privacy," he concluded, "was one of the principal methods used to gain total state control over the German people."

The present-day Soviet Union and People's Republic of China are totalitarian states. These governments place little value on personal privacy. On occasion, they have employed tactics against their citizens similar to those used in Nazi Germany. The USSR and China regard privacy as a relatively unimportant and "bourgeois" concept. Far more important to them is the creation of what they call the "true communist state" and social and economic equality, and to these aims, they believe, all individual rights and considerations must be subjugated.

Professor W. W. Kulski of Syracuse University noted this aspect of totalitarian policy when he wrote in his book, *The Soviet Regime* (1963), that "the totalitarian mind accepts all the means which promise the achievement of its ends. A political democrat," he went on, "is ready to compromise some of his ideal ends for the sake of renouncing means which would involve the sacrifice of human lives or freedom. This is the major moral issue dividing any totalitarian, be he Communist or Fascist, from a genuine democrat."

Two popular and widely-read novels have envisioned totalitarian regimes of the future in which there is no privacy, and in which the regimes maintain total control of their citizens. In Aldous Huxley's *Brave New World* (1932) and George Orwell's *1984* (1949), all people exist for the good of society and there is no individuality.

In the society of *Brave New World*, all babies are born in test tubes and never know their parents. As children, they sleep together on cots in large rooms, where they are subjected to what is called "sleepteaching." During sleepteaching, recordings of messages are played at night, messages that the children absorb subliminally.

During sleepteaching, they receive "at least a quarter million warnings against solitude." They are also taught that "every one belongs to everyone else." Children come to regard people who spend time alone as strange and suspect. Indeed, their lives are so structured and ordered that everyone in the "Brave New World" finds it difficult to imagine what "one *could* do in private." The result is the loss of all feelings of personal worth and freedom.

Everywhere in "Oceania"—the society described in *1984*—there are signs that warn in large letters: "BIG BROTHER IS WATCHING YOU." Oceania, as Orwell imagined it, is an almost completely totalitarian government. "All previous dictatorships," he wrote, "had been half-hearted and only half-efficient."

"Part of the reason for this," Orwell explained, "was that in the past no government had the power to keep its citizens under constant surveillance." But "the invention of print...made it easier to manipulate public opinion, and the film and the radio carried the process further." The stage had been set for total goverment control of its citizens.

It was "the development of television," however, "and the technical advance which made it possible to receive and transmit simultaneously on the same instrument," that made "private life come to an end." From that point on,

> Every citizen, or at least every citizen important enough to be worth watching, could be kept for twenty-four hours a day under the eyes of the police and in the sound of official propaganda, with all other channels of communication closed. The possibility of enforcing not only complete obedience to the will of the State, but complete uniformity of opinion on all subjects existed for the first time.

In the apartment of every "party member"—the elite that governed Oceania and held all the important jobs—there was a "telescreen." The telescreen could not be turned off and could observe what was going on in the apartment at the same time it was broadcasting state propaganda. Out-of-doors there were additional telescreens, and where there were no telescreens there were hidden microphones that overheard conversations.

"It was terribly dangerous," Orwell wrote, "to let your thoughts wander when you were in any public place or within range of a telescreen. The smallest thing gave you away. A nervous tic, an unconscious look of anxiety, a habit of muttering to yourself—anything that carried with it the suggestion of abnormality, of having something to hide."

A party member lived "from birth to death under the eye of the Thought Police." In school, children were taught to watch their parents "night and day for symptoms of unorthodoxy," and given ear trumpets to listen through keyholes.

Life was arranged so that party members had no spare time and were never alone. "To do anything that suggested a taste for solitude, even to go for a walk by yourself, was always slightly dangerous." "Newspeak," the language of the party elite of Oceania, had a word for the desire for privacy—it was "ownlife." "Ownlife" was equivalent to "individualism" and "eccentricity" and was regarded as a thoroughly undesirable trait.

Indeed, Oceania was the complete "information society." Most party members were involved in some sort of information collection or processing. The Thought Police watched for heresy and collected data on subversion and disobedience. Other party members worked in propaganda ministries, turning out falsified news and history books. Yet others were at work on a completely new language that would do away with outlawed concepts such as "liberty" or "freedom," and substitute words with new meanings.

The state of privacy in the United States cannot be compared to privacy in Nazi Germany, the Soviet Union, or to the imaginative societies of Orwell and Huxley. In the United States, there is no deliberate and well-coordinated attempt by government to undermine the privacy of American citizens. But Orwell's and Huxley's books and the examples of totalitarian states do stand as warnings of what can happen if privacy is destroyed.

There can be no doubt, however, that privacy in present-day America is under assault. Modern technology and the complex problems of modern society threaten our privacy and challenge the constitutional and legal safeguards that protect that privacy. There is a trend in the United States, Supreme Court Justice William O. Douglas noted in 1966, "whereby the privacy and dignity of our citizens is being whittled away by sometimes imperceptible steps."

"Taken individually," he continued, "each step may be of little consequence. But when viewed as a whole, there begins to emerge a society quite unlike any we have seen—a society in which government may intrude into the secret regions of a man's life at will."

This book will discuss the assault on privacy in contemporary American society. First, we shall look at the concept of a "right to privacy" and trace the integration of that concept into American law. We shall also look at the safeguards that attempt to protect us from unreasonable searches and seizures by government agents and from wiretapping and electronic eavesdropping.

Two final chapters will deal with the threat to privacy presented by the widespread use of personality tests and lie-detector tests by employers and others, and with the ways in which the computer endangers personal privacy. In his book *The Technological Society* (1964), French social critic Jacques Ellul wrote that "Modern man never asks himself what he will have to pay" for increased technological progress and power. "*This,*" Ellul continued, "is the question we ought to be asking."

It is also a question that this book will ask. Can the privilege of personal privacy be guaranteed in the Computer Age? Only if vigorous measures are taken now, privacy experts tell us, to shore up the right to privacy and keep it abreast of our rapidly changing technology and society. Otherwise, they claim, the price we may have to pay for increased technological prowess will be a tragic loss of personal privacy and individual autonomy.

2
THE RIGHT
TO PRIVACY

The makers of our Constitution
undertook to secure conditions
favorable to the pursuit of happiness....They conferred, as against
the Government, the right to be let
alone—the most comprehensive of
rights and the most valued by civilized man.

>Justice Louis Brandeis
>in *Olmstead* v.
>*United States* (1928)

No one shall be subjected to arbitrary interference with his privacy,
family, home or correspondence,
nor to attacks upon his honour and
reputation. Everyone has the right
to the protection of the law against
such interference or attacks.

>Article 12 of the
>United Nations'
>"Universal Declaration
>of Human Rights"

The Constitution of the United States does not mention the right to privacy. This should not be surprising. America in 1787—the year the Constitution was written—was a large country with a small population. Most Americans lived in small villages or on isolated farms. Moreover, communication and transportation were still primitive. There were no telephones or computers. The electronic revolution in technology was an event to come in the still distant future.

But if the Founding Fathers failed to mention the right to privacy, there are nevertheless strong indications that they regarded it as important. The Declaration of Independence and the Constitution shared three general themes: the worthiness of the individual, the need for limited government, and the importance of private property.

Each of these themes necessarily implied the existence of a right to privacy. Individual worth made little sense unless the individual was protected from outside intrusion and violation. The very purpose behind the idea of limited government was the establishment of a government strong enough to supply adequate order and security, but not strong enough to destroy individual liberty. And private property had little meaning unless it was safe from seizure or confiscation.

CONSTITUTIONAL
GUARANTEES TO PRIVACY

In order to guarantee individual liberty, the Founding Fathers added the first ten amendments to the Constitution. Several of these amendments touch upon the right to privacy.

The First Amendment guarantees the freedom of religion, speech, press, "the right of the people peaceably to assemble," and "to petition the Government for a redress of grievances." Judicial decisions have extended First Amendment guarantees to include the privacy of letters in the mail and the right to join associations without fear of police surveillance, spies, or informers.

In his *Commentaries on the Constitution of the United States* (1833), Supreme Court Justice Joseph Story wrote that the First Amendment was designed to secure the rights of "private sentiment" and "private judgment." Private judgment and sentiment, he believed, were essential to a democratic form of government in which all citizens played a part.

The Third Amendment states that "No soldier shall, in time of peace, be quartered in any house, without the consent of the owner, nor in time of war, but in a manner to be prescribed by law."

The quartering of soldiers in private homes in present-day America seems unlikely. But at the time it was written, the Third Amendment was addressed to a particular grievance—that Americans had been forced to house British soldiers in the days before independence had been won. Clearly, the adoption of this amendment showed that the Founding Fathers regarded privacy as an important right.

The "plain object" of the Third Amendment, wrote Story, was "to secure the perfect enjoyment of that great right of the common law, that a man's house shall be his own castle, privileged against all civil and military intrusion."

Perhaps the strongest Constitutional guarantee of personal privacy was the Fourth Amendment. It protects the people from "unreasonable searches and seizures" of "their persons, houses, papers, and effects." It likewise requires that a warrant be issued by the proper authorities before any search or seizure of personal property be undertaken by law enforcement officials.

According to Justice Story, the Fourth Amendment is "indispensible to the full enjoyment of the rights of personal security, personal liberty, and private property." The key to the amendment, he believed, is a clause that requires that warrants could be granted only on reasonable cause, after swearing on oath, with the exact premises, and the person or objects to be seized clearly stated for all to read.

Judge Thomas Cooley, another prominent nineteenth

century American jurist and author of *Constitutional Limitations* (1868), wrote that the Fourth Amendment grants the "citizen's immunity in his home against the prying eyes of the government."

The Fifth Amendment also provides protection of privacy. It states that "no person ... shall be compelled in any criminal case to be a witness against himself, nor be deprived of life, liberty, or property, without due process of law." This Constitutional guarantee has been called "the right to remain silent."

This amendment was designed to prevent the use of torture to obtain testimony or confession of a crime. In his excellent short book *The 5th Amendment Today* (1955), Erwin Griswold, professor of law at Harvard, pointed out that the Fifth Amendment evolved from the long struggle between individual liberty and the collective power of the state to intimidate and coerce. The Fifth Amendment, he concluded, guaranteed individual liberty in the face of the enormous power of the government.

The Fifth Amendment, Griswold maintained, stressed the privacy and importance of every individual citizen. It extended its protection, he went on, even to "hardened criminals." "We do not make even the most hardened criminal," Griswold concluded, "sign his own death warrant or dig his own grave, or pull the lever that springs the trap on which he stands. We have through the course of history developed a considerable feeling of the dignity and intrinsic importance of the individual man. Even the evil man is a human being."

The Ninth Amendment to the Constitution stated that "The enumeration in the Constitution of certain rights shall not be construed to deny or disparage others retained by the people." This amendment implied that there were other, additional rights that Americans should enjoy not listed in the Constitution or the first eight amendments. It prohibited the federal government from interfering with these rights. Since none of these "additional rights" were named, it was left for later Americans to discover what they were and undertake proper protection of them. Some courts have interpreted "the right to privacy" to be among these unlisted rights.

Thus the First, Third, Fourth, Fifth, and Ninth Amendments guarantee freedom and rights that may imply a right to privacy. But there is also one other amendment, the Fourteenth, adopted in 1868 more than seventy-five years after the first ten, that can be interpreted as implying a right to privacy.

The Fourteenth Amendment states that:

> No state shall make or enforce any law which shall abridge the privileges or immunities of citizens of the United States; nor shall any state deprive any person of life, liberty or property, without due process of law; nor deny to any person within its jurisdiction the equal protection of the laws.

The Fourteenth Amendment was designed to guarantee basic American rights to blacks, who had recently been released from slavery. In recent years, however, the Supreme Court has used the amendment to extend the rights, as listed in the first ten amendments, to the states and to require the state governments to abide by the requirements of the federal Constitution.

THE RIGHT TO PRIVACY
IS DEFINED
FOR THE FIRST TIME
By the end of the nineteenth century, Americans had begun to become concerned about the right to privacy. The population of the nation had grown considerably, from just under 4 million in 1790 to 63 million in 1890. Much of the population was crowded into large and rapidly growing cities such as New York, Philadelphia, and Chicago.

But more significantly, new inventions were revolutionizing the communications industry. The telephone was invented in 1876. By the 1880s, the first cases of wiretapping—eavesdropping on private telephone conversations—had been reported.

The 1880s also saw the invention of instantaneous photography and the Linotype machine. Instantaneous photography dispensed with the need to sit still for a period of time while one's photograph was taken and therefore made it possible to photograph persons without their knowing it. The Linotype machine made the production of newspapers cheaper and more efficient.

On December 15, 1890, an article entitled "The Right To Privacy" appeared in the *Harvard Law Review*. Its authors were two Boston lawyers, Samuel D. Warren and Louis Brandeis. Twenty-six years later, in 1916, President Woodrow Wilson appointed Brandeis to the Supreme Court, where he wrote several important decisions involving the right to privacy.

It is generally accepted that the impetus for the article came from Mr. Warren. Warren's wife was the descendent of a prominent Bostonian family. Accustomed to entertaining lavishly, she was also accustomed to privacy. On at least one occasion, however, a gossipy Boston newspaper printed detailed stories of things that had happened at Mrs. Warren's parties. Both she and her husband resented the fact that intimate details of their private lives had been published openly, without their consent.

"That the individual shall have full protection in person and in property," Warren and Brandeis wrote, "is a principle as old as the common law;* but it has been found necessary from time to time to define anew the exact nature and extent of such protection. Political, social, and economic changes" in society, they explained, "entail the recognition of new rights, and the common law, in its eternal youth, grows to meet the demands of society."

History shows, they went on, that "in very early times" the law protected individuals only from "physical interference with life and property." Liberty simply meant "freedom from actual restraint" and the law regarded one's

---

* The "common law" is a term frequently used to describe the body of law derived from judicial decisions. "Civil law," on the other hand, is primarily legislative in origin. Common law has been called "judge-made law" and is based on court decisions. Civil law (also called statutory law) is codified by a legislative body. Thus the common law may grow and develop according to judicial interpretations in a succession of cases. Civil law can be changed only through laws passed by a legislature. In their article, Warren and Brandeis hoped to appeal to judges and others involved in judicial decisions and convince them that the common law had room for the development of a right to privacy.

property in a purely material sense, as one's "lands and cattle." But as time passed, wrote Warren and Brandeis, this simple materialistic interpretation of life and property changed. As civilization progressed, "there came a recognition of man's spiritual nature, of his feelings, and his intellect."

Slowly, the "scope" of legal rights "broadened." What had once been narrowly-interpreted rights to life and property likewise broadened. The "right to life," they observed, now "has come to mean the right to enjoy life—the right to be let alone." Moreover, they added, "the right to liberty" now includes "the exercise of extensive civil privileges; and the term 'property' has grown to comprise every form of possession—intangible, as well as tangible," material possessions as well as spiritual possessions.

Warren and Brandeis summarized the growth and change of the common law toward a recognition of spiritual possessions:

> *This development of the law was inevitable. The intense intellectual and emotional life, and the heightening of sensations which came with the advance of civilization, made it clear to men that only a part of the pain, pleasure, and profit of life lay in physical things. Thoughts, emotions, and sensations demanded legal recognition, and the beautiful capacity for growth which characterizes the common law enabled the judges to afford the requisite protection, without the interposition of the legislature.*

The authors then declared that "Recent inventions and business methods call attention to the next step which must be taken for the protection of the person, and for securing what Judge Cooley calls the right 'to be let alone.'"

What were the "recent inventions" that threatened privacy? "Instantaneous photographs and newspaper enterprise," Warren and Brandeis claimed, "have invaded the sacred precincts of private and domestic life." The two men believed that conditions had reached a crisis point. Modern technology, they wrote, threatens "to make good the prediction that 'what is whispered in the closet shall be proclaimed from the housetops.'"

"The press is overstepping in every direction the obvious bounds of propriety and of decency," they wrote. "Gossip is no longer the resource of the idle and vicious, but has become a trade, which is pursued with industry as well as effrontery. To satisfy a prurient taste the details of sexual relations are spread broadcast in the columns of the daily papers," they charged. "To occupy the indolent, column upon column is filled with idle gossip, which can only be procured by intrusion upon the domestic circle" by snooping and invasion of privacy.

Warren and Brandeis then summarized the dilemma of individuals in regard to privacy. "The intensity and complexity of life" in the modern, civilized world, they wrote, "have rendered necessary some retreat from the world, and man, under the refining influence of culture, has become more sensitive to publicity, so that solitude and privacy have become more essential to the individual." But at the same time, they went on, "modern enterprise and invention have, through invasions upon... privacy, subjected" modern men and women "to mental pain and distress, far greater than could be inflicted by mere bodily injury."

The authors surveyed the common law tradition, looking for provisions that might be construed as protective of privacy. They found one such provision. "The common law," they noted, "secures to each individual the right of determining, ordinarily, to what extent his thoughts, sentiments, and emotions shall be communicated to others."

"The existence of this right," they went on, "does not depend upon the particular method of expression adopted." Painting, sculpture, music, writing, are all protected. Nor does the right depend upon the quality of the communication, for a "casual letter," a great poem or play, even "a song sung," or "words spoken" are protected equally. "In every such case," the authors concluded, "the individual is entitled to decide whether that which is his shall be given to the public."

Warren and Brandeis noted that in the eighteenth and nineteenth centuries the common law gave protection to communications, because communications were regarded as property. But the two authors were not satisfied with this definition, because they regarded the communications protected by law as more than mere property.

In reality, they concluded, "The principle which protects personal writings and all other personal productions, not against theft and physical appropriation but against publication in any form, is ... not the principle of private property, but that of an inviolate personality."

In common law, they added, "the protection afforded to thoughts, sentiments, and emotions, expressed through the medium of writing or of the arts, so far as it consists in preventing publication, is merely an instance of the enforcement of the more general right of the individual to be let alone."

The common law right of "determining ... to what extent ... thoughts, sentiments, and emotions shall be communicated to others," then, was at bottom a right to an "inviolate personality" and "to be let alone." Or, as the authors called it, "the general right to the immunity of the person—the right to one's personality."

And since the common law does indeed protect communications, Warren and Brandeis continued, then, the "existing law affords a principle which may be invoked to protect the privacy of the individual from invasion either by the too enterprising press, the photographer, or the possessor of any other modern device for recording or reproducing scenes or sounds."

Warren and Brandeis urged the extension of the common law principle covering communications to all threats to privacy in modern life. They also believed that the right to privacy "should receive the added protection of the criminal law," but recognized that inclusion of the right to privacy in criminal law would require legislation.

In conclusion, the two authors told their readers that "the protection of society must come mainly through a recognition of the rights of the individual." Society, they noted, now had in its hands a "weapon" to protect the right to privacy from further erosion. What society must decide, the authors said, was to make use of that weapon.

Society has indeed made use of the "weapon" outlined by Warren and Brandeis. The article stimulated a great deal of discussion and debate in its own time, and still does. Since the article appeared in 1890, its views on privacy have slowly worked their way into common law practice. A majority of states today accept the notion of a right to privacy, and four have adopted legislation covering the right to privacy.

3
THE RIGHT TO PRIVACY IN MODERN AMERICA

This freedom may be termed more accurately "the right to be let alone" or personal autonomy, or simple "personhood." ... An individual should retain the right to engage in any form of activity unless there exists a countervailing state interest of sufficient weight to justify restricting his conduct. This is the essence of personhood; a rebuttable presumption that all citizens have a right to conduct their lives free of government regulation.

Judge J. Braxton Craven, Jr. of the Fourth Circuit Court

$\bigcup$udicial practice in modern America has protected the right to privacy in two general areas of activity. First, it has recognized that an individual may have an interest in avoiding disclosure of personal and confidential matters, and has given American citizens a means to take legal action when they believe their privacy has been violated.

Second, since 1965 the Supreme Court has stated that individuals should have privacy and independence in making certain kinds of intimate decisions. These decisions include contraception, abortion, and other family matters of an extremely personal nature.

Many observers, however, believe that the laws protecting privacy in present-day America are weak and inadequate. Arthur Miller, a professor of law at the University of Michigan, describes privacy laws as "a thing of threads and patches." Another critic has stated that they are in such a state of fluidity and change that they can only be compared to a "haystack in a hurricane," in imminent danger of coming undone and destroyed.

THE RIGHT TO PRIVACY AND
PRESENT-DAY COMMON LAW

The first case regarding the right to privacy to come before a high court was *Roberson* v. *Rochester Folding Box Co.* (1902). Roberson was a young woman who sued a milling company for using her picture, without her permission, in an advertisement to sell flour. Her photograph was printed in an ad under the caption "Flour of the Family."

Chief Justice Parker of the New York Court of Appeals discussed the "right to privacy" in his decision in the case. The right, he explained, was not to be found in the commentaries of the great English jurist, Sir William Blackstone, or in any other commentaries on the law. Indeed, he noted, there was no mention of the right to privacy until 1890, when it was "presented with attractiveness, and no inconsiderable ability" by Warren and Brandeis.

Judge Parker then gave an elegant definition of his own for the right to privacy. "The so-called 'right to privacy' is," he wrote, "as the phrase suggests, founded upon the claim that a man has the right to pass through this world, if he wills, without having his picture published, his business enterprises discussed, his successful experiments written up for the benefit of others, or his eccentricities commented upon either in hand bills, circulars, catalogues, periodicals, or newspapers; and, necessarily, that the things which may not be written and published of him, must not be spoken of him by his neighbors, whether the comment be favorable or otherwise."

The New York Court of Appeals, however, decided against Roberson. The Court declared that it sympathized with her problems and difficulties, but stated that the common law precedents were too vague to establish a right to privacy in this case. The Court called on the New York legislature to pass laws protecting privacy.*

Three years later, in 1905, another privacy case came before a Georgia court. The case involved Paolo Pavesich, who sued the New England Life Insurance Company for using his picture in an Atlanta newspaper advertisement. The ad placed him next to a second figure, an "ill-dressed and sickly looking person," in the words of the court.

Under Pavesich's photograph was the caption that in the "healthy and productive period of life," he bought insurance from New England Life Insurance and was now happy he had done so. The caption under the other picture said that this man had failed to buy insurance when he was well and hardy, and now regretted his improvidence.

Pavesich had never consented to having his picture used in the advertisement. He had never made the statement attributed to him in the caption and had never bought insurance from New England Life Insurance Company.

*The New York legislature responded by passing a privacy law, with interesting results. The law made it a crime and civil wrong to use the name or likeness of a person for "advertising purposes or for purposes of trade." The law was too narrowly-drawn, however, and has been interpreted by New York courts as restricting use of private names and pictures *only* in advertising, leaving them free to be used for other purposes.

In the case of *Pavesich v. New England Life Insurance Company*, Judge Cobb decided in favor of Pavesich. It was the first time an American court had accepted the idea of a "right to privacy." Cobb said that the right to privacy was a "natural right"—a right that can be discerned by reason, even though it is not part of any legal code that has been written down.

"The right of privacy," Cobb noted, "has its foundations in the instincts of nature. It is recognized intuitively, consciousness being witness that can be called to establish its existence." He explained:

> *Any person whose intellect is in a normal condition recognizes at once that as to each individual member of society there are matters private and there are matters public so far as the individual is concerned. Each individual as instinctively resents any encroachment by the public upon his rights which are of a private nature as he does the withdrawal of those rights which are of a public nature.*

"A right to privacy in matters purely private," Cobb concluded, "is therefore derived from natural law."

After the *Pavesich* decision, judicial acceptance of a common law right to privacy became more commonplace. Present-day American courts, wrote William Prosser,* a privacy expert, in the 1960 edition of the *California Law Review*, divide privacy violations into four categories: (1) intrusion upon solitude, seclusion, or private affairs; (2) the public disclosure of embarrassing private facts about an individual; (3) publicity that places a person in a false light in the public eye; and (4) the appropriation of another person's name or likeness for personal advantage.

☐ *Intrusion upon a person's seclusion or solitude.* American courts have come to regard exposure of a person's private activities to public view as disturbing to his or her equanimity, personal calm, composure, and

---

*Prosser is coauthor with John W. Wade of *Materials on Torts*, a widely used and respected guide on law now (1982) in its seventh edition.

evenness of mind. The interest that is protected here is a mental one.

In this category of the right to privacy, the basis for belief that one's privacy has been violated is not the physical harm that may have resulted from the intrusion into one's private affairs. It is the loss of spiritual and emotional well-being that one may have suffered. This category has been primarily used to protect an individual from the activities of private eavesdroppers and wiretappers, and from Peeping Toms.

☐ *Public disclosure of embarrassing facts.* This category allows an individual legal remedy if private facts about him or her are disclosed publicly. Courts have required that the facts be indeed private ones and that they be publicly declared, that is, to a wider public than two or three others.

Even if private facts about an individual are true, they cannot be published unless the person involved agrees to allow them to be published. Nor do the facts have to be damaging to a person's reputation to be actionable in court. They need only to have been private, and regarded by the individual as worthy only of his or her own attention.

☐ *Publicity that places a person in a false light in the public eye.* This category depends upon the falsity of the information publicized. Impersonating another person or forging another's signature are regarded as violations of this category.

☐ *Appropriation of another's name or likeness for one's personal advantage.* The *Pavesich* case, mentioned earlier, is an example of a violation of this category, which attempts to protect an individual from anything that may constitute an attack upon his or her identity.

One successful case tried under this category involved a man whose name and signature were used, without his consent, by a corporation on a telegram sent to a governor to urge passage of a certain bill. Since the man had not known about the use made of his name, the court agreed that his privacy had been violated.

Common law thus does provide some protection of privacy. But the common law protection of the right to privacy has its deficiencies. The interpretation of privacy law differs from state to state and from case to case. No one who brings a privacy case to court can be certain how that case will turn out. Moreover, common law protections of privacy involve only private actions, and not governmental invasions of privacy, under most circumstances.

It is likewise a fact that court actions are expensive, and a person whose privacy has been threatened may not have the time or means to make use of the protections the law provides.

Finally, a court case may mean further public airing of the very information the person regards as private and confidential, leading him or her to avoid legal action that may result in additional publicity of private matters.

THE SUPREME COURT
AND PRIVACY

In the 1965 case of *Griswold* v. *Connecticut*, the Supreme Court for the first time explicitly defined and accepted the right to privacy. At issue was an 1879 Connecticut law that made it a crime for anyone—including married couples— to use contraceptives of any kind. The law also stated that anyone who "assists, abets, counsels, causes, hires, or commands another to use contraceptives" could be prosecuted and punished.

On two earlier occasions the Supreme Court had declined to consider the validity of the Connecticut law. In 1943, a Connecticut physician had asked the Court to knock down the law because it prevented him from prescribing contraceptives to women whose lives might be endangered by child bearing. The Court dismissed the case because the physician, a Dr. Tileson, could not show that he was personally harmed by the law. In 1961, the Court once again dismissed a challenge to the law, arguing a "lack of justiciable controversy," since no one had ever been tried for violating the law.

Opponents of the law brought a third case before the Court. This time they made certain that they had a defendant who had been arrested for violating the law, and therefore had been personally harmed by its existence. The defendant was Mrs. Estelle Griswold, the Executive Director of the Planned Parenthood League of Connecticut, located in New Haven. A second defendant was Dr. Buxton, a professor at the Yale Medical School and the Medical Director of the League.

On November 1, 1961, Mrs. Griswold and Dr. Buxton had opened the birth control clinic in New Haven. On November 10, the two were arrested and fined $100 for giving information on birth control to married persons. Both Griswold and Buxton openly admitted that they had distributed the information. Their convictions were upheld by two Connecticut courts before the case found its way to the Supreme Court.

Justice William O. Douglas wrote the decision for the Court. Douglas noted that several widely accepted rights had not been expressly written into the Constitution. Among these unwritten rights, he wrote, were the "freedom to associate," "the right to distribute printed material," and "freedom of inquiry."

Even though these rights were not mentioned in the Constitution, Douglas continued, "the First Amendment has been construed to include" them. The First Amendment's guarantee of freedom of the press, he pointed out, includes not only the simple right of being able "to print," but has been extended to include the "right to distribute," "the right to receive," and "the right to read" printed material. Similarly, he went on, the freedom of speech encompasses not only the right "to utter," but also the "freedom of inquiry," "the freedom of thought," and the "freedom to teach."

The Supreme Court, Douglas explained, has included these unmentioned "peripheral" rights under the protection of the First Amendment, so that the specific guarantees of free speech and press would be more secure and certain. Without the peripheral "right to distribute," he added, the freedom of the press would have little meaning. Without freedom of thought and inquiry, the freedom of speech would be superfluous.

Douglas found the Supreme Court's protection of the "freedom to associate" and of "privacy in one's association" particularly significant. The right of association, he wrote, is not mentioned in the Bill of Rights, but the Court has nevertheless declared that it exists, because it is implied by the First Amendment's guarantee of the "right to assembly."

Furthermore, Douglas went on, the Court has likewise extended the "right to assembly" to include "the right to believe, to express one's attitudes or philosophies by membership in a group or by affiliation with it or by other lawful means," even though these rights are not mentioned in the First Amendment. Thus the "specific guarantees in the Bill of Rights," Douglas concluded, "have penumbras, formed by emanations from those guarantees that help give them life and substance."

Douglas then turned to the right of privacy. The "penumbras" and "emanations" of the guarantees of the Bill of Rights, he claimed, create "zones of privacy." One zone of privacy, he explained, is created by the First Amendment's guarantee of the "right to associate" free of government intrusion. Another zone of privacy, he added, is established by the Third Amendment's prohibition of the quartering of troops in a private home.

Douglas found other zones of privacy in the Fourth Amendment's protection against "unreasonable searches and seizures;" in the Fifth Amendment's guarantee of a "right to silence;" and in the Ninth Amendment's protection of the rights "retained by citizens."

The Connecticut anti-contraception law, Douglas concluded, violated the zones of privacy established by the Bill of Rights. The Connecticut law, he claimed, was too broad and sweeping. It granted the state too much power to intrude into personal matters and took away basic rights that belonged to the individual. "Would we allow the police," Douglas asked, "to search the sacred precincts of marital bedrooms for telltale signs of the use of contraceptives? The very idea is repulsive to the notions of privacy surrounding the marriage relationship."

The privacy of marriage, Douglas concluded, is one area of privacy "that must be protected from government intrusion." For in marriage, he wrote:

—— 35

> *We deal with a right of privacy older than the Bill of*
> *Rights—older than our political parties, older than*
> *our school system. Marriage is a coming together for*
> *better or for worse, hopefully enduring, and intimate*
> *to the degree of being sacred. It is an association that*
> *promotes a way of life, not causes; a harmony in living,*
> *not political faiths; a bilateral loyalty, not commercial*
> *or social projects. Yet it is an association for as noble*
> *a purpose as any involved in our prior decisions.*

Justice Douglas was joined in his opinion by Chief Justice
Earl Warren and two other associate justices. Three justices, Arthur Goldberg, Byron White, and John Harlan,
agreed that there was a right to privacy, but disagreed
with Douglas's method of locating that right in the "penumbras" and "zones of privacy" created by the Bill of Rights.
Justices Hugo Black and Potter Stewart dissented from the
others' opinions.

Justice Goldberg wrote that the right to privacy was
so essential that it could be ranked among those rights the
Supreme Court regarded as "so rooted in the traditions
and conscience of our people as to be ranked as fundamental."

The right to privacy, he went on, could be protected
by law even though "it is not guaranteed in so many words
by the first eight amendments." Goldberg stressed the sig-
nificance of the Ninth Amendment's protection of "certain
rights . . . retained by the people" from government intrusion. Surely, he concluded, a "right so basic and fundamental and so deep-rooted in our society as the right of
privacy in marriage is included in the Ninth Amendment's
protection."

Justice White likewise agreed that there was a right
to privacy. But he believed that right should always be
balanced with a state's right to intrude upon personal privacy in exceptional situations. In this case, he wrote, the
state of Connecticut had not shown any justification for
invading the privacy of married couples, and the anticontraception law should be held unconstitutional.

Justice Harlan believed that the right to privacy should
be included among those rights and basic values "implicit

in the concept of ordered liberty." He believed that the Connecticut law was unconstitutional because it denied the right of "due process" of law guaranteed in the Fourteenth Amendment.

In their dissent, neither Justice Black nor Justice Stewart could find the right to privacy in the Constitution or the Bill of Rights. "There are, of course," Black wrote, Constitutional guarantees "which are designed in part to protect privacy at certain times and places with respect to certain activities."

But there was no general guarantee of the right to privacy, he declared, nor was there any provision in the Constitution that might abridge or limit the privacy of individuals. "I like my privacy as well as the next one," he explained, "but I am nevertheless compelled to admit that government has a right to invade it unless prohibited by some specific constitutional provision."

Black lamented that the Court had written the right to privacy into the law of the land in the *Griswold* decision. What bothered him, he said, was that the term "privacy" was a "broad, abstract and ambiguous concept" that could be interpreted in many different ways.

Justice Stewart believed that the Connecticut anticontraception law was "uncommonly silly" and "obviously unenforceable." But he did not believe that it violated the Constitution. "I can find no such general right of privacy in the Bill of Rights," he concluded, "or in any case ever before decided by this Court."

Following the *Griswold* case, the Supreme Court has mentioned the right to privacy on several occasions, the most important of which were the abortion decisions of 1973. The two cases, *Roe* v. *Wade* and *Doe* v. *Bolton*, came from Texas and Georgia, states where restrictive abortion laws prevented women from obtaining abortions except under extreme conditions. "Roe" and "Doe" were fictitious names, used to protect the privacy of the women who were challenging the abortion laws in their states.

By a decision of 7 to 2, the Supreme Court struck down the abortion laws in both Texas and Georgia. Justice Harry Blackmun wrote the decision for the Court. "The Constitution," he noted, "does not explicitly mention any right to privacy." But in a "line of decisions," he went on, "the Court has recognized that a right of personal privacy, or a guarantee of certain areas or zones of privacy, does exist under the Constitution."

Blackmun maintained that only those personal rights that could be called "fundamental" or "implicit in the concept of ordered liberty" should be included under the guarantee of personal privacy. These areas of fundamental right to privacy, he said, were marriage, procreation, family relationships, and child-rearing and education.

Blackmun believed that the right to privacy was implied in several parts of the Constitution—in the First, Fourth, and Ninth Amendments, and elsewhere. But he concluded that it was in the Fourteenth Amendment's concept of personal liberty that freedom "broad enough to encompass a woman's decision whether or not to terminate her pregnancy" could be found.

The section of the Fourteenth Amendment Blackmun believed conferred the right to privacy in abortion decisions stated that "No State shall make or enforce any law which shall abridge the privileges or immunities of citizens of the United States." It also guaranteed all citizens the right to "due process" and the "equal protection of the laws."

Blackmun concluded that a woman had a right to terminate her pregnancy, if she made a personal decision to do so. The state, he added, could not make or enforce any law that would abridge that right.

But Blackmun did not believe that a woman's right to privacy on the question of abortion was an absolute right. There are times, he wrote, when a state may intrude upon a woman's privacy and "may properly assert important interests" in preventing abortions. Blackmun maintained that during the first trimester (the first three months of pregnancy), a woman could decide to terminate her pregnancy and the state could not interfere with that right. But in the second trimester—a period when medical statistics showed that a mother was more likely to be harmed physically by an abortion—government had the right and "compelling interest" to regulate abortions in order to protect the health of the mother. In the third trimester, Blackmun concluded, medical science has determined that a fetus can live outside of its mother's womb. Thus the state, he argued, has a right to outlaw abortions in this period, except in cases where the mother's health is threatened by the pregnancy.

Justice Potter Stewart, who had dissented in the *Griswold* decision and claimed that he could find no right to privacy in the Constitution, now sided with Blackmun against the abortion laws. The Court recognizes, he wrote, "the right of the *individual*, married or single, to be free from unwarranted governmental intrusion into matters so fundamentally affecting a person as the decision whether to bear or beget a child."

Quoting an earlier Supreme Court decision, Stewart added that we must look upon liberty as "a rational continuum which, broadly speaking, includes a freedom from all substantial arbitrary impositions and purposeless restraints... and which also recognizes, what a reasonable and sensitive judgment must, that certain interests require particularly careful scrutiny of the stated needs asserted to justify their abridgment."

Justice Douglas believed that a "woman is free to make the basic decision whether to bear an unwanted child. "Elaborate argument," he continued, "is hardly necessary to demonstrate that childbirth may deprive a woman of her preferred life-style and force upon her a radically different and undesired future." The only occasions, Douglas concluded, when the "State has interests to protect" and can make laws for or against abortion are when the life and health of the mother are involved, or when it can be determined that the fetus is alive and can live independently of the mother.

Two justices, Byron White and William Rehnquist, issued vigorous dissents to the majority opinion. White had supported the majority in *Griswold* and defended the existence of a right to privacy in that case. In the abortion decision, however, he wrote that "the Court simply fashions and announces a new constitutional right for pregnant mothers and, with scarcely any reason or authority for its actions, invests that right with sufficient substance to override most existing state abortion statutes."

"The Court," White went on, "apparently values the convenience of the pregnant mother more than the continued existence and development of the life or potential life which she carries." There was no "constitutional warrant," he claimed, "for imposing such an order of priorities on the people and the legislatures of the States." Decisions about abortion laws, he concluded, should not be made by the courts, but "should be left with the people and to the political processes the people have devised to govern their affairs."

Justice Rehnquist also rejected the arguments of the majority. "I have difficulty," he wrote, "in concluding, as the Court does, that the right of 'privacy' is involved in this case." Like White, he believed that abortion was a legislative matter, not a judicial one. It would have been better, he concluded, if the Court had refrained from imposing its views on abortion on the rest of the country.

Twentieth century American legal practice has woven a web of law that protects the right to privacy. Common law allows Americans to sue for damages when they believe their privacy has been violated. The Supreme Court has declared that certain intimate matters, such as contraception and abortion, should remain free from government intrusion.

Many observers, however, believe that this web of protection for privacy is inadequate. Privacy, they point out, is still not truly regarded as a basic and fundamental right. It does not have the status of "freedom of religion" or the "freedom of the press." Privacy laws vary from state to state and are extremely susceptible to the variations and uncertainties of judicial interpretation and the whims of judges and juries.

The problem, the critics believe, is that the Supreme Court has produced no solid underlying theory concerning the right to privacy. In the *Griswold* decision on the Connecticut contraception law and in the abortion decisions, the Court arrived at no general definition of the right to privacy. Nor were the nine justices able to agree on how that right can be derived from the Constitution.

In *Griswold*, there were four separate opinions among those who wanted to strike down the Connecticut law and who defended the existence of a right to privacy. Justice Douglas described "zones of privacy" protected by the Constitution. Justice Goldberg wrote of the Ninth Amendment as a basis for the right to privacy. Justice White claimed that the right to privacy did indeed exist, but said that it had to be balanced with the government's right to intrude upon personal privacy in exceptional circumstances. Justice Harlan based the right to privacy on the Fourteenth Amendment's "due process" clause and described it as a basic right "implicit in the concept of ordered liberty."

The two dissenters in *Griswold*, it will be remembered, totally rejected the notion of a right to privacy based upon the Constitution. One of them, Hugo Black, one of the most highly regarded justices of the twentieth century, found the concept of a right to privacy vague and nebulous. He feared that the Court had greatly distorted the Constitution by trying to find guarantees for a right to privacy hidden somewhere among the Constitution's sentences and clauses.

Nor did the abortion decision help to clear things up. Once again, there was disagreement among the seven justices who voted to strike down the abortion laws and no consensus on what the right to privacy involves or on how it is based on the Constitution. Once again, too, two dissenters strongly protested the majority opinion and believed that the Court had decided wrongly.

Privacy advocates claim that the Supreme Court's confusion on the right to privacy has made the status of that right in present-day American law precarious and uncertain. They believe that the Court must sort out its own thoughts and beliefs on privacy before privacy law can become more secure. Only when the Court has established the nature of the right to privacy and its basis in constitutional law, they conclude, can it then decide just what is protected (or not protected) under the right to privacy.

4
SEARCHES
AND SEIZURES:
PART I

The right of the people to be
secure in their persons, houses,
papers, and effects, against unreasonable searches and seizures,
shall not be violated, and no warrants shall issue, but upon probable cause, supported by oath or
affirmation, and particularly describing the place to be searched,
and the persons or things to be
seized.

The Fourth Amendment to the
United States Constitution

P

erhaps the most flagrant abuse of the right to privacy is breaking and entering. Consider these two examples:

☐ At ten o'clock in the morning of January 9, 1973, fifteen well-armed police officers smashed the front door and broke into the home of the Pine family. The three members of the family—Mr. and Mrs. Pine and their thirteen-year-old daughter, Melody—were at home. Mr. Pine, who worked nights, was asleep upstairs. Mrs. Pine and Melody were downstairs in the living room.

A few of the police held Mrs. Pine and Melody at gunpoint, forcing them to remain seated on a living room couch. Others ran upstairs where they awakened Mr. Pine and kept their guns trained on him.

The terror continued for fifteen minutes, until the police discovered the true name of the family. When the name "Pine" was supported by identification cards presented by Mr. and Mrs. Pine, the fifteen officers left the house. The people they had wanted to arrest lived next door.

☐ The story of the Conforti family of Massapequa, New York, is even more striking. One evening, two agents from the Federal Bureau of Narcotics and Dangerous Drugs knocked on the Conforti door and declared that they had a warrant that permitted them to search for $4 million that was supposed to be hidden somewhere on the Conforti property. The agents said that the money had been taken from the sale of illegal drugs.

John Conforti explained that he knew nothing about the money and did not sell illegal drugs. But the two agents nevertheless entered the house, along with twenty other men. For twenty-four hours, the agents smashed furniture, ripped up walls, tore up the backyard patio, and dug holes in the lawn in search of the money, which was not found. They left the Conforti home in shambles.

Conforti was a roofing contractor and a respected businessman in his community. He had never been arrested. But his wife's brother, Louis Cirillo, had been. Cirillo had recently been convicted of selling narcotics and police had found nearly $1 million buried in his backyard. An unidentified informer had told police that another $4 million would be found at the Conforti home.

Frank Monastero, the regional director of the Bureau of Narcotics and Dangerous Drugs, found no reason to apologize for the actions of his agents. In an interview with *Time* magazine, he declared that his men had acted reasonably. "We didn't send a lot of guys in with instructions of 'you pound here' and 'you pound there,'" he explained. "We went through a series of progressive steps. Whether or not this was reasonable is up to the courts to decide. I personally felt that it was."

Each year, similar searches and seizures occur throughout the United States. Usually, they are carried out by over-zealous police officers or federal agents who believe they are on the track of genuine criminals. In this chapter, we shall look at what protections American law provides for such intrusions of personal privacy.

PRIVACY AND
SEARCH WARRANTS
The modern practice of issuing search warrants dates from a 1765 case in England, at a time when the American colonies were still under British rule. In the case of *Entick* v. *Carrington*, an English court forbade the use of "general warrants" that allowed government agents to search private premises for any incriminating evidence they might find.

General warrants, the court declared, lack specifics and allow government agents too much leeway to violate private property. "By the laws of England," it added, "every invasion of private property, be it ever so minute, is a trespass." To be legal, the court concluded, warrants had to state the specific evidence that the government agents wanted to find.

The Fourth Amendment of the Constitution, ratified in 1791, guaranteed the "right of the people to be secure...against unreasonable searches and seizures." The amendment was directed against a particular grievance that had arisen in the 1760s and 1770s when British soldiers used general warrants to search the homes of colonists for smuggled goods.

The Fourth Amendment defined a reasonable search as one in which there was "probable cause" that incriminating evidence would be found. The amendment also required that warrants be issued only upon "oath and affirmation," and that the warrant "particularly" describe "the place to be searched, and the persons or things to be seized."

In the landmark 1886 case *Boyd* v. *United States*, the Supreme Court further defined what was meant by a legal search warrant. In this case, a man named Boyd had been charged under a provision of the Federal Customs Act. The provision required that he produce his business papers in court, or else be found guilty of smuggling charges that had been brought against him.

For Boyd, it was a no-win situation. If he turned over the papers, they could be used against him in court. If he did not turn over the papers, he would automatically be charged with the crime. He took his case to the Supreme Court, believing that his rights had been violated.

The Supreme Court agreed. The Court declared that the requirement that the papers be turned over was a violation of Boyd's Fourth Amendment right that protected him against unreasonable searches and seizures. The Court likewise believed that Boyd's Fifth Amendment right, guaranteeing that he not be "a witness against himself," protected him from producing evidence that could be used against him.

There is an "intimate relation" between the Fourth and Fifth Amendments, Justice Joseph Bradley explained, so that they "run almost into each other." Both amendments, he went on, "apply to all invasions on the part of the government and its employees of the sanctity of a man's home and the privacies of life."

"It is not the breaking of his doors, and the rummaging of his drawers," Bradley concluded, "that constitutes the essence of the offense; but it is the invasion of his indefeasible right of personal security, personal liberty and private property.... Any forcible and compulsory extortion of a man's own testimony or of his private papers to be used as evidence to convict him of crime or to forfeit his goods is within the condemnation" of the Fourth and Fifth Amendments. To seize Boyd's papers or effects without a proper warrant, the Court explained, amounted to forcing him to testify against himself—and therefore such warrantless searches are a violation of the defendant's Fourth and Fifth Amendment rights.

THE EXCLUSIONARY RULE

In the 1914 case of *Weeks* v. *United States*, the Supreme Court took another major step toward protecting American citizens from unreasonable searches and seizures. The *Weeks* decision developed what is known as the "exclusionary rule," which forbids the use of any evidence in federal courts that was obtained in violation of the Fourth Amendment. If evidence in a federal court trial can be shown to have been obtained illegally—by unreasonable searches and seizures—then that evidence is to be *excluded* from the trial proceedings, even if it means that a criminal might go free.

"The Fourth Amendment," the Court declared, "... put the courts of the United States and Federal officials, in the exercise of their power and authority, under limitations and restraints." Moreover, the Court went on, the same amendment did "forever secure the people, their persons, houses, papers and effects against all unreasonable searches and seizures under the guise of law."

Federal officials, the decision stated, must not be allowed to resort to violations of Fourth Amendment rights in order to obtain evidence of criminal wrong-doing. The Court explained:

If letters and private documents can thus be seized and held and used in evidence against a citizen accused of an offense, the protection of the Fourth Amendment declaring his right to be secure against such searches and seizures is of no value, and, so far as those thus placed are concerned, might as well be stricken from the Constitution. The efforts of the courts and their officials to bring the guilty to punishment, praiseworthy as they are, are not to be aided by the sacrifice of those great principles established by years of endeavor and suffering which have resulted in their embodiment in the fundamental law of the land. . . ."

In conclusion, the Court stated that the exclusionary rule clearly meant that "conviction by means of unlawful seizures and enforced confessions . . . should find no sanction in the judgments of the courts." Without this protection of individual privacy, the Court added, the Fourth Amendment would be reduced to "a form of words" void of meaning and substance.

The *Weeks* decision excluded the use of illegally obtained evidence from *federal* courts. In 1961, forty-seven years later, in the landmark case of *Mapp* v. *Ohio*, the Supreme Court extended Fourth Amendment rights to cases before state courts.

The case began on May 23, 1957, when three Cleveland police officers arrived at the home of Dollree Mapp. They had received information that a person was "hiding out in the home who was wanted for questioning about a recent bombing." The officers knocked on Mapp's door and demanded entrance. Mapp, however, called her attorney and refused to admit the police without a search warrant. The officers advised headquarters of the situation and began surveillance of the house.

Three hours later, after four more police officers arrived on the scene, the police once again demanded entrance. Miss Mapp at first did not come to the door, and the police forced their way into the house. Sometime later Mapp's attorney arrived, but the police would not let him see his client or enter the house.

Mapp had been halfway down the stairs from the upper floor when the police broke in. She immediately asked to see a search warrant and was shown a piece of paper by an officer. Mapp grabbed the paper and attempted to conceal it on her person. A struggle followed, and the police regained the piece of paper, which was not a warrant.

Mapp was handcuffed and taken upstairs, where the policemen proceeded to search her possessions. They searched a dresser, a chest of drawers, a closet, and some suitcases. The rest of her residence was also searched. In the course of the search, obscene literature was found and seized by the police. Mapp was later convicted of possession of this literature, described as "lewd and lascivious books and pictures."

Dollree Mapp complained that her rights as a citizen of the United States had been violated and she took her case to the Supreme Court. The question before the Court was clear: Did the Fourth Amendment's prohibition of unreasonable searches apply to this case and should the evidence obtained in the search therefore be excluded from a state court because it had been illegally obtained?

In a 5 to 4 decision, the Court held that the evidence had been obtained illegally and should be excluded. Justice Tom Clark wrote the opinion for the majority. The "right to privacy" protected by the Fourth Amendment, he wrote, is extended to the states by the Fourteenth Amendment, which states that no state shall "deprive any person of life, liberty, or property, without due process of law." The evidence against Mapp, he maintained, had been "secured by official lawlessness in flagrant abuse" of basic rights. Clearly, he concluded, Mapp had been denied "due process of law."

The states must be required to exclude illegally obtained evidence from state trials, Clark added, because to do otherwise would tend "to destroy the entire system of constitutional restraints on which the liberties of the people rest." The exclusion doctrine, he said, was "an essential part of the right to privacy." As things now stand, Clark continued, "a federal prosecutor may make no use of evidence illegally seized, but a State's attorney across the street may, although he supposedly is operating under the enforceable prohibitions of the same Amendment."

By allowing illegally obtained evidence to stand in trial, Clark noted, the states encourage "disobedience to the Federal Constitution." This encouragement to violate the Fourth Amendment, he believed, must be eliminated. "Nothing can destroy a government more quickly," he explained, "than its failure to observe its own laws, or worse, its disregard of the charter of its own existence," its Constitution.

"The ignoble shortcut to conviction left open to the State," Clark stated, "tends to destroy the entire system of constitutional restraints on which the liberties of the people rest." He stated:

> *Having once recognized that the right to privacy embodied in the Fourth Amendment is enforceable against the States, and that the right to be secure against rude invasions of privacy by state officers is, therefore, constitutional in origin, we can no longer permit that right to remain an empty promise.... Our decision, founded on reason and truth, gives to the individual no more than that which the Constitution guarantees him, to the police officer no less than that to which honest law enforcment is entitled, and, to the courts, that judicial integrity so necessary in the administration of justice.*

THE REQUIREMENTS
FOR WARRANTS

The Fourth Amendment prohibits "unreasonable" searches and seizures. In the *Boyd* decision, the Supreme Court condemned unreasonable invasions of the "indefeasible right of personal security, personal liberty and private property." In the *Weeks* and *Mapp* cases, it excluded all evidence from federal and then from state courts that had been obtained as the result of unreasonable searches and seizures. But what is meant by "unreasonable"?

American law regards a *reasonable* search and seizure as one that follows the procurement of a proper warrant. A proper warrant, the Supreme Court has said, must be issued by a public official—a judge or a magistrate—who is clearly empowered to issue warrants. Warrants must distinctly specify the *place* that will be searched. They must likewise specify the *purpose* of the search and the *object* or *objects* that are to be seized.

Police officers must also show *probable cause* before they are granted a warrant. Probable cause is shown, the Supreme Court has declared, not by a mere statement that "affiants have received reliable information from a credible person," but by showing *how* the information was received and *why* the person who conveyed the information is to be trusted. Probable cause also means that police officers must show *what* they expect to find as a result of the search. There must be probable cause to believe that a crime is being carried out on the premises in question, and that evidence will be found there that proves the crime.

Police may request *arrest* warrants or *search* warrants, but whatever kind of warrant they receive, it must be dated at the time of issuance and specific time limits must be set on how long the warrant is valid. There are exceptions to the restrictions placed on warrants. A police officer may search premises without a warrant if he or she believes that there is no time to obtain a warrant because of fear that evidence may be destroyed, because the situation at hand is an emergency (for example, the search of an armed suspect), or when the police officer is in "hot pursuit" of a suspected criminal.

In this chapter, we have looked at Fourth Amendment safeguards for privacy and traced their development to the present day. In the *Boyd* decision, we found that the Court believed that a warrantless search and seizure of a person's property could amount to a violation of Fourth and Fifth Amendment rights. In the *Weeks* and *Mapp* decisions, we saw that the Court ordered all evidence that had been obtained illegally as the result of warrantless searches and seizures to be excluded from all federal and state courts.

The Fourth Amendment provides significant protection from governmental intrusions upon privacy. An area left uncovered by the Amendment, however, is *private* intrusions upon personal privacy. For example, if a landlord should search your apartment, or a co-worker your desk at work, the search is not protected by the Fourth Amendment. If the landlord or co-worker finds evidence of wrongdoing, that evidence can be turned over to the authorities and used against you in court.

The Constitution and American legal practice have created a strong network of protection against intrusions of privacy. A proper search warrant, issued by a judge or magistrate, is needed before government officers invade the privacy of our homes. In the next chapter, we shall look at a number of cases in which the Supreme Court struggled with the definition of Fourth Amendment rights. In many of these cases, the Court came down firmly on the side of privacy rights. In others, it suspended those rights and granted police or other government officers the right to conduct warrantless searches and seizures, and to intrude upon personal privacy under certain circumstances.

5
SEARCHES AND SEIZURES: PART II

The poorest man may, in his cottage, bid defiance to all the forces of the Crown. It may be frail; its roof may shake; the wind may blow through it; the storm may enter; the rain may enter; but the King of England may not enter; all his force dares not cross the threshold of the ruined tenement.

A statement by the eighteenth century English statesman, William Pitt, describing the common law belief that a "man's home is his castle."

$\mathcal{S}$upreme Court doctrine involving search warrants is one of the most complex areas of law. Even legal experts find it difficult to figure out under which circumstances a police officer may conduct a search and seizure without a warrant, or when that officer must have a warrant to make the search and seizure legal.

The Supreme Court's difficulty arises from the choice it must make in each individual case. In some cases, violations of Fourth Amendment privacy rights may be plain to see. But in others, there may be a fine line between Fourth Amendment rights and a police officer's need to uncover criminal activity and capture evidence that will lead to the conviction of those responsible for it.

This chapter will explore Supreme Court decisions in four areas where the Court's doctrine on warrants has been subject to variation and intricacy: (1) warrantless searches following an arrest; (2) warrantless administrative searches; (3) warrantless searches in what lawyers call "exigent circumstances"; and (4) warrantless searches of automobiles and moving vehicles.

In deciding cases in these areas, the Court must ask itself two difficult questions. First, how can the Court uphold individual privacy and Fourth Amendment rights and assure that "a man's home is his castle"? And second, how can it reach a decision that does not unduly hamper police work and make it unreasonably hard for the police to apprehend wrong-doers? Clearly, the Court must be hard-pressed at times to strike a balance between these two needs and problems of American society.

WARRANTLESS SEARCHES
FOLLOWING AN ARREST

A warrantless search may follow a legal arrest. The Supreme Court regards this invasion of privacy as reasonable because (1) a police officer, for his or her own protection, must discover if the prisoner is armed with a deadly weapon, and (2) it may be necessary to prevent the prisoner from disposing of evidence under his or her immediate control. For a more extensive search, a warrant is required.

Most Americans would deem these two conditions for warrantless searches as permissible and necessary. At the same time, however, there can be no doubt that the right to warrantless searches is subject to abuse. An over-zealous police officer, for example, may look for grounds for arrest simply in order to conduct a search. And if the arrest is judged in court to have been legal, then the search will likewise be held to have been legal and any evidence that was seized will be admissible in the trial.

The Court has addressed the problem of warrantless searches following arrests on many occasions. We shall look at two cases in which contrasting decisions were reached.

In the 1947 case of *Harris* v. *United States*, the Supreme Court upheld a warrantless police search. After obtaining a warrant for Harris's arrest on charges of check forgery, police officers entered the apartment of the suspect. The arrest was made, followed by a thorough search of Harris's four-room apartment. The police hoped to recover two checks involved in the forgery.

In the course of the search, a police officer discovered a sealed envelope marked "George Harris, personal papers" inside a desk drawer. The envelope contained altered selective service documents, the possession of which is a federal offense. Harris was later convicted of illegal possession of the documents.

When the case came before the Supreme Court, a majority of the justices declared that the police had acted correctly. "The Fourth Amendment," the majority opinion stated, "has never been held to require that every valid search and seizure be effected under the authority of a search warrant."

In this case, the Court noted, the police agents had entered the apartment in possession of a lawful warrant for arrest. In the process of a "valid search," they had found material—the selective service documents—"of which the government was entitled to possession." "Search and seizure incident to lawful arrest," the Court concluded, "is a practice of ancient origin and has long been an integral part of law-enforcement procedures of the United States and of the individual states."

Justice Felix Frankfurter, however, strongly dissented and was joined in his dissent by two other justices. "Because I deem the implications of the Court's decision to have serious threats to basic liberties," he wrote, "I consider it important to underscore my concern over the outcome" of this case. The majority decision, he warned, "permits rummaging throughout a house without a search warrant on the ostensible grounds of looking for the instruments of a crime for which an arrest, but only an arrest, has been authorized."

"The prohibition against unreasonable search and seizure is normally invoked by those accused of crime," he went on, "and criminals have few friends." But the Fourth Amendment was not written simply to protect criminals, he said. It was also written to secure the privacy of all Americans from encroachment by government officials.

If the police are granted the right to search and seizure without a proper warrant that so specifies, he added, then it is a license to violate laws that should be basic to every American. "The implications of such encroachment," he concluded, "reach far beyond the thief or the black marketeer" to every American citizen.

In the *Harris* case, the Court allowed an extensive search of a four-room apartment following a lawful arrest. Twenty-two years later, however, in the 1969 case of *Chimel* v. *California*, the Court took notice of Frankfurter's dissent in *Harris* and severely tightened the standards under which police may conduct warrantless searches following arrests.

On September 13, 1965, three police officers presented themselves at Chimel's Santa Ana, California, home. They were admitted to the house by Chimel's wife and waited fifteen minutes for her husband to return from work. When Chimel arrived, they presented him with a warrant for his arrest for the burglary of a coin shop.

Over Chimel's objections, the police conducted a search of the large, three-bedroom house. They had no search warrant. In the course of the search numerous coins, medals, and other items were discovered and later used as evidence to convict Chimel of burglary.

Chimel took his case to the Supreme Court, charging that his Fourth Amendment rights had been violated. The Court agreed. There was ample justification, the Court said, for police officers to search the person and immediate area around a prisoner—the area in which "he might gain possession of a weapon" or destroy evidence.

"There is no comparable justification, however," the Court continued, "for routinely searching any room other than that in which an arrest occurs—or, for that matter, for searching through all the desk drawers or other closed or concealed areas in that room itself. Such searches...may be made only under the authority of a search warrant...."

The Court concluded that the evidence against Chimel had been illegally obtained and was therefore inadmissible in court. In the *Chimel* case, the Court struck a new balance between an individual's right to privacy and the police officer's need to conduct searches. After *Chimel*, police officers could not use the arrest of an individual in his or her home as an excuse to conduct a wide-ranging search of that home.

WARRANTLESS
ADMINISTRATIVE
SEARCHES
In certain situations regarded as emergencies, the Supreme Court has allowed warrantless searches by administrative officers such as health or revenue officers. Health officers, for example, may seize and destroy milk from cows that have not been vaccinated for tuberculosis, in order to prevent the sale of that milk to the public. Revenue agents may seize a person's property for failure to pay taxes, on the grounds that payment of taxes is necessary to keep the government running.

In the 1959 case of *Frank* v. *Maryland*, the Supreme Court upheld the right of a Baltimore health inspector to conduct a warrantless search of a private residence he regarded as dangerous to public health. The case arose when the health inspector was looking for the cause of extreme rat infestation in a residential area of the city. One house particularly bothered him. It was in extremely run-down condition and belonged to a Mr. Frank. When he looked around the outside of the property, the inspector found it covered with trash and garbage and saw evidence of rats.

Mr. Frank suddenly appeared and asked the inspector what right he had to be on his property. The inspector explained his reasons for being there and asked to see Frank's basement. Frank refused. The inspector returned the next afternoon, accompanied by Baltimore police officers. He knocked on Frank's door, but received no response. He then again examined the run-down state of Frank's house and the accumulation of garbage. Later, Frank was arrested for violating provisions of the city code intended to promote public health.

In a close 5 to 4 decision, the Court decided that the Baltimore official had acted correctly. Justice Frankfurter wrote the decision for the Court. The city of Baltimore, he concluded, had the right to maintain minimum standards of well-being for the community, and this right superseded Frank's right to privacy.

Frank, he added, simply did not have "the absolute right to refuse the consent for an inspection designed and pursued solely for protection for community's health." Baltimore's inspection standards, Frankfurter noted, had been established "with due regard for every convenience of time and place" and had not put an intolerable burden upon Frank.

Four justices disagreed. "The Fourth Amendment," Justice Douglas wrote in his dissent, "was designed to protect the citizen against uncontrolled invasion of his privacy." The amendment, he noted, "does not make the home a place of refuge from the law," but it does require a legal warrant before the "privacy" of a home "may be invaded."

"We live in an era," Douglas went on, "when politically controlled officials have grown powerful through an ever increasing series of minor infractions of civil liberties.... The same pattern appears over and again whenever government seeks to use its compulsive force against the citizen. Legislative committees ... fire marshalls ... police ... sometimes seek to place their requirements above the Constitution."

"We cannot do less," Douglas concluded, than require that a health inspector have a warrant before he enters the premises, "and still be true to the command of the Fourth Amendment which protects even the lowliest home in the land from intrusion on the mere say-so of an official."

The *Frank* decision had ruled that warrantless searches by administrative officials were permissible under certain emergency situations. In the 1967 case of *Camara* v. *Municipal Court of the City and County of San Francisco*, however, the Supreme Court overturned that decision. At issue was a private citizen, Camara, who had been arrested and convicted for refusing to allow a warrantless search of his residence by a public building inspector.

Camara believed that his Fourth Amendment privacy rights had been violated, and the Court agreed. In an opinion delivered by Justice Byron White, the Court stated that under the Fourth Amendment Camara did indeed have a constitutional right to demand that building inspectors have a search warrant before entering his home. The Court had adopted Justice Douglas's dissenting opinion in the *Frank* case, in which he had insisted that administrative searches be conducted only after the issuance of a proper warrant.

In a second decision, *See* v. *City of Seattle*, handed down the same day as the *Camara* decision, Justice White declared that Fourth Amendment warrant requirements would also apply to administrative searches of business premises. In both the *Camara* and *See* decisions, White indicated that the requirements governing the issuance of warrants in housing and business inspections would be less strict than those governing the issuance of criminal warrants. But he insisted that warrants would be necessary.

Four years later, however, the Court seemed to reverse itself again. In the case of *Wyman* v. *James* (1971), Justice Harry Blackmun, writing the majority opinion, upheld the constitutionality of a statute that permitted a caseworker to enter the home of a welfare recipient against her will. A warrantless search was possible, Blackmun wrote, even though the caseworker had no cause to believe that a crime had been committed or was being committed on the premises.

The *Wyman* decision reflected the growing conservatism of the Court after a peak period of liberalism in the 1960s. In *Camara* and *See*, the Court had tilted toward increased support for Fourth Amendment rights. In *Wyman*, it tilted the other way, toward making administrative searches easier for social workers involved in the exercise of their duties. Since the *Wyman* decision, the Court has continued to favor the needs of administrators carrying out warrantless searches.

WARRANTLESS SEARCHES
UNDER EXIGENT
CIRCUMSTANCES

In its review of cases, the Supreme Court will sometimes declare that "exigent circumstances"—urgent circumstances that require immediate action—justify warrantless searches and seizures. At other times, the Court will find that circumstances regarded by a police officer as urgent were not urgent at all, and admonish the officer for not taking time to obtain a proper warrant.

In the 1948 case of *Johnson* v. *United States*, for example, a narcotics agent smelled opium and believed that the smell was coming from a hotel room he had just passed. Without waiting to obtain a warrant, he entered the room and found opium and an opium-burning device.

The narcotics agent arrested a suspect, who was later convicted. The suspect, a man named Johnson, charged that the evidence used against him at his trial—the opium and opium-burner—had been illegally obtained, and therefore could not be used against him. He likewise charged that the agent had had no grounds for obtaining a proper warrant, even if he had tried to obtain one.

The Supreme Court agreed that the search and seizure of the evidence had been illegal. There had been sufficient time to obtain a warrant, the Court noted, but none was obtained. Under the exclusionary rule, the evidence was inadmissible. But the Court believed that a warrant could have been issued, if the agent had taken time to get one. The smell of opium, the Court concluded, "might very well be found to be evidence of the most persuasive character" in allowing a legal search to take place.

"Crime, even in the privacy of one's own quarters," the Court declared, "is, of course, of grave concern to society . . . but the right of officers to thrust themselves into a home is also a grave concern," a grave concern "not only to the individual but to a society which chooses to dwell in reasonable security and freedom from surveillance" and government intrusion. The smell of opium did not justify the officer's quick response and individual action. "When the right of privacy must reasonably yield to the right of search, is, as a rule," the Court stated, "to be decided by a judicial officer, not by a policeman or governmental agent."

In the 1967 case of *Warden* v. *Hayden*, the Court found that exigent circumstances justified a warrantless search. In this case, police officers entered a house they were told an armed robber had entered less than five minutes earlier. During their search, they found and seized weapons and clothing that were later used as evidence to convict the criminal. Most of the search and seizure was carried out before or simultaneous with the arrest of the suspect.

Were the search and seizure constitutional? The Court said that they were. "The Fourth Amendment," the Court stated, "does not require police officers to delay in the course of an investigation if to do so would gravely endanger their lives." In this case, the Court explained:

> Speed . . . was essential, and only a thorough search of the house for persons and weapons could have insured that Hayden was the only man present and that police had control of all weapons which could be used against them or to effect an escape.

A highly controversial Supreme Court decision involving exigent circumstances was *Schmerber* v. *California* (1966). In this case, following an automobile accident, Schmerber was under the care of doctors at a hospital. Over Schmerber's protests, the police directed the doctors to conduct a blood test. Schmerber's blood showed a blood-alcohol content of 0.18 percent. In California, a level of 0.15 percent is considered proof of drunkenness.

Schmerber was arrested and convicted of drunk driving. Believing that his Fourth and Fifth Amendment rights had been violated, he took his case all the way to the Supreme Court. In a 5 to 4 decision, the Court declared that the blood test had been conducted constitutionally and that Schmerber's rights had not been violated.

Justice William Brennan wrote the majority opinion. Schmerber's Fifth Amendment rights had not been violated, he argued, because Schmerber had not been forced to give "personal communication or testimony" against himself. The extraction of blood from Schmerber's veins, he explained, was "performed in a reasonable manner" and did not amount to self-incrimination.

Brennan likewise claimed that Schmerber had not been denied his Fourth Amendment rights, even though no warrant had been issued that permitted a "search" of Schmerber's blood. A warrantless search was permissible in this case, he stated, because (1) the police had "plainly probable cause" to arrest and charge Schmerber and (2) the police could reasonably assume that unless they took immediate action, the evidence against Schmerber would no longer be at hand. Brennan feared that during the time it took the police to acquire a proper warrant, Schmerber's natural body mechanisms would lower the level of alcohol in the blood. In these urgent circumstances, he concluded, the Constitution "does not forbid the States minor intrusions into an individual's body...."

Four vigorously dissenting opinions were issued. Justice Hugo Black believed that Schmerber's Fifth Amendment rights had been clearly violated. "To reach the conclusion," he wrote, "that compelling a person to give his blood to help the state convict him is not equivalent to compelling him to be a witness against himself strikes me as quite an extraordinary feat." The framers of the Constitution, he said, had intended the Fifth Amendment to protect the people from occasions of "governmental oppression" such as forced blood tests.

Justice Douglas believed that the blood test was unconstitutional because it violated Schmerber's "zone of privacy." One year earlier, in the landmark *Griswold* v.

Connecticut decision, Douglas had written about "zones of privacy" protected by the Constitution.* The government, he now argued in the *Schmerber* case, had no right to invade the privacy of Schmerber's body to obtain a blood test over Schmerber's protests and without a proper warrant.

Justice Abe Fortas found a different reason for dissenting in the *Schmerber* decision. The government, he wrote, did not have the right to "commit any kind of violence upon the person... and the extraction of blood, over protest, is an act of violence."

As the *Johnson, Warden,* and *Schmerber* cases reveal, Supreme Court justices may differ widely on the question of warrantless searches under exigent circumstances. When exigent circumstances are involved, the Court decides each case on its own merits, and it is difficult to predict when the Court will come down on the side of individual privacy and the protection of Fourth Amendment rights, or when it will opt to grant police the right to warrantless searches.

WARRANTLESS SEARCHES OF AUTOMOBILES AND MOVING VEHICLES

In the 1964 case of *Preston* v. *United States*, the Supreme Court held the warrantless search of an automobile to be unconstitutional. The car in question was locked in a police garage at the time of the search. Since there was no cause to believe that the car would be taken out of the hands of the police, the Court believed that there had been ample time to obtain a warrant before the search was conducted.

When an automobile is in motion, however, the Court has taken a different view on warrantless searches and privacy rights. A moving vehicle, once stopped by the police, might be moved from police supervision before a warrant could be issued.

Two 1973 Supreme Court decisions upheld warrantless searches. In the case of *United States* v. *Robinson*, the Court maintained that a warrantless search of a driver's body and his car following an arrest for a routine traffic

---

*See Chapter Three, pp. 35-36 for Douglas's statements on "zones of privacy."

violation was constitutional. In the case of *Gustafson* v. *Florida*, the Court found that a warrantless body search of a suspect was legal under certain circumstances.

Gustafson was arrested for driving his car without a license. After taking Gustafson into custody, the arresting officer conducted a search of Gustafson's body and found a package of cigarettes that he believed contained marijuana. He took the evidence into his possession and it was later used against the unlucky suspect.

Gustafson sued, claiming that his rights had been violated. The Supreme Court disagreed. In a majority decision written by Justice William Rehnquist, the Court's most conservative member, the Court said that the policeman "was entitled to make a full search of the suspect's person." He was likewise entitled, the Court added, to seize evidence he found as "fruits, instrumentalities, or contraband" indicative of criminal conduct.

Privacy experts found the Court's decisions in *Robinson* and *Gustafson* wrong-headed and a threat to the right to privacy. An automobile, they argued, should be regarded as a private place and be subject to the same Fourth Amendment warrant requirements that apply to a private home.

Privacy experts feared that the Court's decisions in *Robinson* and *Gustafson* would allow police to arrest a person for running a red light or a traffic sign, and then conduct searches and seizures in violation of privacy rights. "Privacy rights are in trouble," noted William Petrocelli, a former assistant attorney general of California, "when failure to carry a driver's license can justify a full body search to find a couple of joints."

The Fourth Amendment protects Americans from "unreasonable searches and seizures." A long series of Supreme Court decisions have reinforced that right and carefully defined the circumstances under which warrants are required before the privacy of one's home or property can be violated. No right to privacy enjoyed by Americans has been more rigorously maintained than the "right of the people to be secure...against unreasonable searches and seizures."

Of course, Fourth Amendment rights are not absolute. No right is. On occasion, the standards employed to protect our privacy must bow to the needs of law enforcement and police investigation. The genius of our system of government is that those standards are the responsibility of the courts, and not the police. Police officers can— and do—err in the performance of their duties, but their errors can—and have been—brought to task by the courts.

This chapter and the previous one discussed restrictions on *physical* intrusion of privacy by government agents. It was this kind of intrusion—searches and seizures of "persons, houses, papers, and effects"—that the Founding Fathers had in mind when they added the Fourth Amendment and the other protections of the Bill of Rights to the Constitution in 1791. In the following two chapters, we shall see how the Supreme Court has expanded the traditional meaning of the Fourth Amendment (and the other constitutional protection of privacy) to cover invasions of privacy by electronic eavesdropping devices, wiretaps, and other modern inventions unknown to the authors of our Constitution.

6
THE EAVES-DROPPERS: PART I

The proper posture of democratic man is surely not that of a snooper crouching over a recording device listening to the intimate and private conversations of two individuals. When we recognize fully the moral degradation created by our own involvement in these practices, our courts will exclude this type of evidence once and for all.

> Norman Redlich in *Confronting Injustice, The Edmond Cahn Reader* (1966)

One device in particular deserves particular attention. Wiretapping, that sneaky business that has become a plaything in America—especially in the government—during the past few years, has become a term on the tongue of every American....I have become convinced that its rampant use is not consonant with a free society.

> Former Senator Sam Ervin of North Carolina (1968)

E̲ach year, law enforcement officials carry out approximately 600 authorized wiretaps in the United States. Most of these are done by the Federal Drug Enforcement Administration and by authorities concerned with organized crime and other forms of criminal activity. No one knows how many illegal and warrantless wiretaps are made each year by government officials.

No one knows, either, how many wiretaps are carried out each year by private investigators and private businesses. Most often, private wiretapping involves family problems. Husbands or wives may hire investigators to pry into the affairs of their spouses. In other instances, parents have asked that telephones used by their children be tapped.

Private businesses tap company telephones to see if employees are involved in theft or some other dishonest activity. On occasion, one company may have the telephones of a rival company tapped to see what business plans and ventures the rival is undertaking. Labor unions have tapped the telephones of management representatives during labor disputes, and management has tapped the telephones of labor leaders.

"Bugs" are electronic devices used to overhear and record private conversations. No one knows how widespread their use is, but many observers believe that "bugging" is at least as widespread as wiretapping. Privacy experts regard bugging as commonplace within and between corporations. Recent advances in microtechnology have produced bugs that are smaller and more powerful than ever before— and therefore easier to use and install.

In this chapter and the next, we shall look at the types of wiretaps and bugs available today, and at the attempts that have been made, through government regulations and by the courts, to bring their illegal use under control.

THE KINDS OF WIRETAPS

The tapping of telephone lines has become very sophisticated. Numerous private investigators are skilled in wiretapping and their services are available for a fee. There are also government agents who specialize in wiretapping. In addition, wiretapping devices are on sale at specialty shops and are available to the general public.

The following is a survey of the kinds of wiretaps now in use:

☐ The simplest type of wiretap is made on the telephone line between the telephone and the telephone pole. An FM transmitter is used to carry the conversation from the tap to a voice-activated tape recorder located somewhere nearby.

☐ Another type of wiretap is installed at the terminal box found on a telephone pole near the telephone to be tapped. The tap is then routed to any other line in the area. This wiretap is similar to what happens when a person hires an answering service to handle his or her calls.

☐ A third type of wiretap is called "blue-streak" monitoring. Blue-streak monitoring is done with the cooperation of the telephone company. Law enforcement officials first contact a telephone company executive, usually a vice-president. The officials present the executive with a warrant that lists the telephone number to be tapped. The executive then informs the telephone company's "Chief Special Agent" that a wiretap has been requested, and the Chief Special Agent issues an order to the company's switching office, instructing telephone company employees to submit to the warrant.

The employees connect a device known as a "blue streak" to the line that is to be tapped. The "blue streak" is powered by telephone company power and therefore does not drain power from the tapped telephone. There is no click or other sound that might arouse suspicion. Law enforcement officials can then dial a number (not the number of the telephone being tapped) and be connected to the telephone they want to listen in on. A voice-activated recorder is attached to the line to record conversations.

☐ There are also transistor-powered wiretaps that can be used to transmit telephone messages to receivers located nearby. Some of these devices do not need to be connected to the telephone. The only requirement is that they be close enough to the line to pick up the electrical signals that radiate from the wires they travel along.

One of these devices is the extremely sensitive "telephone induction coil" that does not need direct contact with the telephone. Conversations can be picked up ten inches away. The coil is used to record conversations in telephone booths.

These devices also include the "clamp-on telephone induction coil" that records both sides of the conversation and also the number that was dialed; the "automatic telephone-line interceptor" that is activated by the telephone call, records both sides of the conversation, and then shuts itself off; and the "hook switch bypass" that records the conversations on the telephone, as well as other conversations in the room where the telephone is located. There are also devices that record numbers dialed, but not the conversations themselves.

☐ In some cases, listening to telephone calls requires no wiretapping at all. This is especially true of long-distance calls. Most long-distance calls today are no longer carried over wires, but are transmitted through the air by microwave—from microwave tower to microwave tower—across the world. Conversations carried by microwave can be overheard by a system known as "plucking." In his book *Technospies* (1978), the journalist and lawyer Ford Rowan discussed the technique of plucking. "A person with an instruction manual and a few thousand dollars' worth of equipment," Rowan wrote, "can build an antenna to listen and record the phone conversations being relayed on microwave."

"It is easy," Rowan claimed, "to find the fixed channel communications of organizations that have leased specific phone lines, organizations like federal government agencies and big corporations." It would be only slightly more difficult, he added, "to intercept direct-dialed phone calls, the kind you make to your mother, your girl friend, or your bookie."

Rowan cited a secret study by the Mitre Research Corporation that discussed the "strategies and techniques that can be employed to intercept communications." The secret study explained how to wiretap conventional telephone lines. It also explained how to intercept microwave transmissions. Only "a moderate amount of knowledge and expertise," it said, "would be required to analyze the radio path, find and install the interception site, and utilize the interception equipment." Furthermore, the study concluded, "the risk of being discovered is fairly low."

Rowan pointed out that much of this new technology was developed by governmental agencies like NSA (National Security Agency), the country's largest intelligence-gathering branch. The technology was developed to keep watch on all Russian activities throughout the world, but once the technology had been developed, Rowan noted, it was available to other branches of the federal government that might want to take advantage of it.

In his book *Privacy, How to Protect What's Left of It*, privacy expert Robert Ellis Smith described how sophisticated the technology is that allows us to listen to microwaves. It is now possible, he wrote, to connect microwave listening devices to computers. The computers are then programmed to respond to certain dialed telephone numbers and record the ensuing conversation. Computers, Smith continued, can also be programmed to key phrases—like the names of drugs—or to voice prints of certain individuals. Once the computer "hears" these phrases or voices, it will record the conversation and store the recording for later use.

"The technology exists," Smith concluded, "for listening to thousands of telephone and room conversations, recording them at a remote location without detection, screening the conversations for key words and for particular individuals . . . all without human intervention."

THE SPECIES OF "BUGS"

There are a wide range of bugs on the market, and they are available to the general public.

☐ A number of electronic listening devices are attractive to eavesdroppers because of their small size. There is "the martini-olive microphone" that is installed in the olive in the drink, with the toothpick used to disguise the aerial. Its range is short—about fifty feet—so that the receiver and recorder have to be located nearby.

There are also wristwatch microphones, tie-clip microphones, tie-pin, cufflink, buttonhole, and fountain pen microphones. There are desk-pen microphones, desk calendar microphones, and "sub-miniature surveillance microphones," which the manufacturer claims are small enough to fit into the cavity in a tooth.

☐ The "shotgun" microphone can record conversations from the vibrations of sound on a wall. Shotgun microphones have a range of 3,500 feet and can also pick up sound through a window. The "doppler radar microphone," by picking up the vibrations on a car window, can record conversations that take place in an automobile.

☐ A "mike and wire" system can be placed in a wall and allows an eavesdropper to listen at some distance from a bugged room. It takes time to install, however, because all traces of the installation must be concealed.

☐ The "listenback" or "keep-alive" makes use of the telephone. The device is installed in the phone. The eavesdropper can then go to another location and dial the telephone's number. When someone answers the phone, the "listenback" is activated and remains activated after the telephone has been returned to the hook.

☐ One of the most common electronic eavesdropping devices is the "infinity transmitter" or "harmonica bug." It uses the telephone as a transmitter of conversations, and can transmit conversations it hears to any other telephone in the world.

The "infinity transmitter" is installed in the telephone in the room to be bugged. The eavesdropper then goes elsewhere and calls the telephone number of the bugged phone. But before the telephone rings, a series of musical tones from a toning device activates the "infinity transmitter" and prevents the phone from ringing. Conversations carried on in the room where the bugged phone is located can then be overheard and recorded.

☐ Modern technology has also developed anti-bugging devices and anti-recording devices. They can easily be concealed on a person or in a room and will prevent any bugs located nearby from transmitting a clear record of a conversation.

EAVESDROPPING:
AN EARLY HISTORY
The earliest cases of wiretapping involved telegraph lines. Telegraph wiretapping was carried on in the 1840s and 1850s. During the Civil War, both sides tapped the telegraph lines of the other to keep track of enemy plans and troop movements.

Telephone wiretapping dates from the 1880s. The two most frequent users of telephone wiretaps in these early years were police officers conducting criminal investigations and stockbrokers trying to obtain secret information on stock deals.

One of the earliest government investigations of wiretapping occurred in 1916. According to the May 17, 1916, *New York Times*, "the Thompson Committee investigating public utilities heard yesterday that the police of New York have been tapping telephone wires by wholesale, and the Committee will begin today an investigation of the entire subject." The *Times* story went on to say that "an official of the New York Telephone Company told Senator Thompson that in the past two years 350 telephone wires have been officially tapped by the police." Senator Thompson's investigation of wiretapping, however, came to an end in 1917 when the United States entered World War I and the attention of the country turned elsewhere.

The official position of the federal government at this time was against wiretapping. In the early 1920s, an attorney general of the United States declared the practice unlawful, and J. Edgar Hoover, who was appointed Director of the FBI in 1924, publicly said that he regarded wiretaps as a "cowardly" way to do police business. In 1928, President Calvin Coolidge reaffirmed the ban on wiretaps.

Also in 1928, the Supreme Court handed down its first decision to deal with the tapping of telephone lines. The case was *Olmstead* v. *United States*. The defendant was Roy Olmstead, a former Seattle, Washington, police lieutenant, who carried on an illegal business dealing in the bootlegging of smuggled liquor.

Olmstead's business was highly lucrative, and he and his associates enjoyed a yearly income of more than $2 million—an enormous sum at the time. But federal agents learned of Olmstead's activities. Over a period of several months, they gathered information on his business by wiretapping his telephones. The wiretaps were made without trespassing on the private property of Olmstead or the people he dealt with. But they were nevertheless in violation of a Washington state law, passed in 1909, that made wiretapping a crime. On the basis of the evidence gathered by wiretap, Olmstead was convicted of violating the National Prohibition Act of 1919, which made it a federal offense to deal in alcoholic beverages. Olmstead drew a sentence of four years at hard labor and a fine of $8,000.

Believing that his rights had been violated, Olmstead took his case all the way to the Supreme Court. But to no avail. In a landmark 5 to 4 decision, the Court decided against him. William Howard Taft, the Chief Justice and a former president of the United States, wrote the opinion for the Court.

Taft denied that the Fourth Amendment's prohibition of searches and seizures could apply in the *Olmstead* case. "There was no searching," he wrote. "There was no seizure. The evidence was secured by the use of the sense of hearing and that only. There was no entry of the houses or offices of the defendants."

"By the invention of the telephone fifty years ago, and

its application for the purpose of extending communications," Taft continued, "one can talk with another at a far distant place." However, Taft added, the language of the Fourth Amendment "can not be extended and expanded to include telephone wires reaching to the whole world from the defendant's house or office."

Taft also denied that the Fifth Amendment was applicable. "There was no evidence," he wrote, "of compulsion to induce the defendants to talk over their many telephones." Rather, "they were continually and voluntarily transacting business without knowledge of the interception." No one had been forced to testify against himself.

Taft added that Congress, by legislation, could "protect the secrecy of telephone messages by making them, when intercepted, inadmissible in evidence in federal criminal trials. . . ." But he believed that the Supreme Court was helpless to deal with the problem, because the Court should not be in the business of "attributing an enlarged and unusual meaning to the Fourth Amendment." He concluded:

> *The reasonable view is that one who installs in his house a telephone instrument with connecting wires intends to project his voice to those quite outside, and that the wires beyond his house and messages while passing over them are not within the protection of the Fourth Amendment. Here those who intercepted the projected voices were not in the house of either party to the conversation.*

Four justices dissented from the views of the Chief Justice. Justice Oliver Wendell Holmes, one of the most widely respected justices to sit on the Court, pointed out that the evidence used to convict Olmstead had been obtained by an illegal act of wiretapping, in direct violation of state law in Washington.

By accepting such illegally obtained evidence, the Supreme Court and the federal government had announced that they would support police officials who broke the law—and would continue to support and pay them in the future. "For my part," he concluded, "I think it a less evil that some criminals should escape than that the government should play an ignoble part."

Justice Butler dissented for another reason. "Telephones are used generally for transmission of messages concerning official, social, business and personal affairs," he wrote, "including communications that are private and privileged—those between physician and patient, lawyer and client, parent and child, husband and wife." For the sake of privacy, he concluded, wiretapping should not be encouraged.

But the most blistering dissent in the *Olmstead* case came from Justice Louis Brandeis, who along with Charles Warren had coauthored the 1890 article on "the right to privacy." Brandeis agreed with Holmes that the federal government should not be in the habit of sanctioning the violation of law in order to obtain evidence.

But Brandeis went further. He believed that the Fourth and Fifth Amendments should apply to the case. When the two amendments were adopted, he noted, it was true that they applied to the techniques used, by governments of the time, to invade an individual's privacy. "Force and violence," he wrote, "were then the only means known to man by which a government could directly effect self-incrimination." A government could torture and it could seize evidence by unreasonable searches and seizures.

However, to limit the prohibitions of the Fourth and Fifth Amendments to these kinds of activities, Brandeis argued, was to deny that times change and the needs of people change. "Subtler and more far-reaching means of invading privacy have become available to government," he pointed out. "Discovery and invention have made it possible for the government, by means far more effective than stretching upon the rack, to obtain disclosure of what is whispered in the closet."

"The progress of science in furnishing the government with means of espionage," Brandeis went on, "is not likely to stop with wiretapping."

He continued:

Ways may some day be developed by which the government, without removing papers from secret drawers, can reproduce them in court, and by which it will be enabled to expose to a jury the most intimate occurrences of the home. Advances in the psychic and related sciences may bring means of exploring unexpressed beliefs, thoughts and emotions. . . . Can it be that the constitution affords no protection against such invasion of individual security?

It was "immaterial" in the *Olmstead* case, he concluded, that the wiretaps had been made without physical intrusion of the property of the defendant. It was also immaterial, he added, that the wiretaps had been made in the name of law enforcement. What was material, he believed, was that the right to privacy of the defendant—even though he was guilty of a crime—had been violated, and violated by a government willing to commit a crime of its own in order to gather information.

Brandeis denounced the government's action.

Experience should teach us to be most on our guard to protect liberty when the government's purposes are beneficent. Men born to freedom are naturally alert to repel invasion of their liberty by evil-minded rulers. The greatest dangers to liberty lurk in insidious encroachment by men of zeal, well-meaning, but without understanding.

Decency, security, and liberty alike demand that government officials shall be subjected to the same rules of conduct that are commands to the citizen. In a government of laws, existence of the government will be imperiled if it fails to observe the law scrupulously.

Our government is the potent, the omnipresent teacher. For good or for ill, it teaches the whole people by its example. Crime is contagious. If the government becomes a lawbreaker, it breeds contempt for law . . . it invites anarchy. To declare that in the administration of the criminal law the end justifies the means—to declare that the government may commit crimes in order to secure the conviction of a private criminal—would bring terrible retribution. Against that pernicious doctrine this court should resolutely set its face.

Brandeis had powerfully stated the conflict between the rights of the individual to privacy and the need of law enforcement officials to gather evidence, and had come down firmly on the side of the individual. In his dissent he was joined by one other justice, Harlan F. Stone. A majority of five on the Court had come down on the side of law enforcement.

"Had the Brandeis analysis prevailed," William Beany, a legal scholar, has pointed out, "all government intrusions on a person's privacy at home, in his papers, and effects, and on his free movement would have had to be justified, with the government forced to bear the burden of showing why a particular form of interference was reasonable. Privacy, though not an absolute, would have a high place in the hierarchy of protected values."

7
THE EAVES-DROPPERS: PART II

I believe that, under the Fourth Amendment, the "sanctity of a man's house and the privacies of life" still remain protected from the uninvited intrusion of physical means by which words within the house are secretly communicated to a person on the outside. A man can still control part of his environment, his house; he can retreat thence from outsiders, secure in the knowledge that they cannot get at him without disobeying the Constitution. That is still a sizeable hunk of liberty—worth protecting from encroachment. A sane, decent, civilized society must provide some such oasis, some shelter from public scrutiny, some insulated enclosure, some enclave, some inviolate place which is a man's castle.

Circuit Judge Jerome Frank, dissenting opinion, *United States* v. *On Lee* (1951)

In the *Olmstead* decision, Chief Justice Taft, writing for the majority, declared that a message traveling along a telephone wire was not protected by the Fourth Amendment. The Fourth Amendment, he reasoned, protected material and tangible things—persons, houses, papers, and effects—and a telephone conversation was not a material and tangible thing.

But Taft suggested that if the government wanted to make wiretapping illegal, it could do so by legislative statute. Since the *Olmstead* decision was handed down in 1928, a series of government directives and congressional laws have attempted to deal with the problem of electronic eavesdropping. During the same period, the Supreme Court has altered its original position and come to regard private conversations as protected by the Fourth Amendment.

FROM *OLMSTEAD* TO *KATZ*

Following the *Olmstead* decision, Attorney General William D. Mitchell declared that government wiretaps could be made only with the approval of or "at the personal direction of the Chief of the Bureau involved." Mitchell also recommended that Congress respond to the *Olmstead* decision with legislation of its own on wiretapping.

In 1934, six years after *Olmstead*, Congress passed the Federal Communications Act (FCA). Section 605 of the Act was directed against wiretapping. It provided that "no person not being authorized by the sender shall intercept any communication and divulge or publish the existence, contents, substance, purport, effect, or meaning of such intercepted communications to any person...."

In the case of *Nardone* v. *United States* (1937), the Supreme Court, basing its decision on Section 605 of the FCA, held that wiretapping by federal officers as well as private citizens was unlawful. The *Nardone* decision likewise banned in federal courts the use of evidence secured by federal agents by wiretapping. In a second *Nardone* decision in 1939, the Court extended the ban to evidence discovered as a result of a wiretapped conversation, but which was not part of the conversation itself.*

In practice, however, wiretapping and electronic eavesdropping continued. The Department of Justice and the FBI interpreted the restrictions of Section 605 in their own self-interest. The wording of Section 605, they argued, forbade the interception *and* the divulgence of communications intercepted by wiretapping. This meant, they concluded, that the Justice Department and the FBI could wiretap as long as the information gathered as a result of the wiretap was not divulged to any person that was not a government employee.

Other loopholes in Section 605 were found. State courts regarded Section 605 as a purely federal statute and admitted wiretap evidence in trials. In practice, too, federal agents continued to use wiretaps if any one of the participants in a conversation, sender or receiver, gave his or her permission for the wiretap.

Another loophole was national security. The coming of World War II saw an increase in electronic surveillance and eavesdropping. Fears that Nazi sympathizers were at work in the United States and that pro-German saboteurs might cause damage to the nation's industries led President Franklin Roosevelt to permit electronic eavesdropping in cases where national security was involved.

A presidential memorandum signed by Roosevelt on May 21, 1941, read:

> *You are therefore authorized and directed in such cases as you may approve, after investigation of the need in each case, to authorize the necessary investigating agents that they are at liberty to secure information by listening devices directed to the conversation or*

---

*The *Nardone* decisions did not overturn *Olmstead*. Both *Nardone* decisions rested on Section 605 of the FCA. It was this statute, the Court said, that was violated when the wiretappings took place. Wiretapping was illegal, but not unconstitutional. In the *Nardone* cases, the Court did not direct its attention to the question of whether or not wiretapping constituted a violation of the Fourth Amendment, but only to the question of a violation of Section 605 of the FCA.

other communications of persons suspected of subversive activities against the government of the United States, including suspected spies.

The memorandum was directed to FBI Director Hoover and to other government officials involved with national security. Roosevelt added that the investigations were to be limited to a "minimum" and, as much as possible, to "aliens" residing in the United States. Director Hoover interpreted the memorandum liberally and permitted his agents to use wiretaps as long as they were approved by him. The agents were allowed to use other electronic listening devices at their own discretion.

In the 1942 case of *Goldman* v. *United States*, the Supreme Court upheld the use of electronic eavesdropping devices, just as fourteen years earlier, it had found wiretaps constitutional. In the *Goldman* case, federal officers listened to a private conversation by attaching a "detectaphone" to the outside wall of a room where the person under surveillance was located.

The Court stated that no Fourth Amendment violation had taken place because there had been no physical invasion of the suspect's property. Goldman's office had not been trespassed upon in order to attach the listening device. Electronic eavesdropping could take place, the Court concluded, as long as the privacy of an individual was not tangibly violated.

After World War II, the Cold War aroused new fears of foreign subversion. At the same time, a rapidly growing crime rate contributed to concerns about law and order. Presidents Truman and Eisenhower renewed Roosevelt's 1941 memorandum and electronic surveillance was used against suspected foreign agents, as well as against American communists and others regarded as subversive. The FBI expanded the use of wiretaps and bugs against suspected criminals.

By the 1950s, however, there were signs that the public and Congress were growing uneasy with widespread wiretapping and electronic surveillance. In 1954, Senator Patrick McCarren of Nevada introduced a bill in Congress that would have outlawed all wiretapping by private investigators, and required a court-order for all wiretaps done by law enforcement officials. A strong anticommunist, McCarren nevertheless did not believe that police or the FBI needed the right to conduct electronic eavesdropping at will.

In 1955, two news stories broke that revealed how widespread wiretapping had become. First, reporters in New York City learned of "a central wiretap station" that could monitor over 100,000 telephone lines in mid-Manhattan. The station had been set up by private investigators.

Next, reporters in Nevada found that rooms in brothels in the state had been wired to record information that could be used against the brothel's clients. The two stories were widely discussed in the press and led to editorials calling for laws and other measures restricting wiretapping and electronic eavesdropping. The stories were only two among many that the press uncovered in the 1950s and 1960s.

In two significant decisions, *On Lee* v. *United States* (1952) and *Lopez* v. *United States* (1963), however, the Supreme Court continued to uphold electronic surveillance as constitutional. In the case of *On Lee*, a government agent hid a radio transmitter in the coat of Chin Poy, an acquaintance of On Lee. The transmitter's antenna was hidden in Chin Poy's sleeve.

Chin Poy then entered On Lee's laundry and began a conversation with his acquaintance. While they talked, their conversation was transmitted to the government agent, who was a federal narcotics officer. Evidence of narcotics trafficking was obtained and later used to convict On Lee. But On Lee took his case to the Supreme Court, believing that the evidence against him had been obtained illegally.

The Supreme Court did not agree. Justice Robert Jackson wrote the opinion for the Court. Chin Poy, Jackson pointed out, had entered On Lee's laundry with Lee's permission. There had been no forced entry or physical intrusion and therefore no direct violation of the Fourth Amendment.

Furthermore, Jackson continued, the use of the electronic listening device likewise did not constitute a violation of the Fourth Amendment. The use of a radio transmitter, he said, was no different from the use of other devices that improved the human senses, like "bifocals," "field glasses," or a "telescope." Indeed, he concluded, On Lee's conversation could have been overheard by the narcotics agent if that agent had been stationed outside an open window. Whether agents used their own ears to gather evidence or were aided by electronic devices, the result was the same and no law had been broken.

Justices Felix Frankfurter and Harold Burton dissented. In cases such as *On Lee*, Burton wrote, the Court must draw a line between a society's need to catch criminals and the protection of an individual's Fourth Amendment rights. In its *On Lee* decision, he concluded, the Court had leaned too far in the direction of law enforcement and had diminished individual rights.

Justice Frankfurter likewise feared that the *On Lee* decision gave government agents too much power. We have no way of knowing, he noted, what future developments in technology may bring. He believed that the Court should have decided against warrantless electronic surveillance in *On Lee*, in order to set a precedent against the use of bugs to invade personal privacy.

In the case of *Lopez* v. *United States*, a hidden pocket recorder was used to record a conversation Lopez had with an Internal Revenue agent. The agent pretended to go along with a bribe Lopez was offering him to avoid payment of taxes. The recording was used to convict Lopez of bribery. A majority of 6 to 3 on the Supreme Court upheld the Lopez conviction. There had been no illegal search and seizure of Lopez's property, they said, and the use of the hidden tape recorder was within the limits allowed by the law and the Constitution.

The majority believed that Lopez had taken a "risk" in offering the bribe, a "risk that the offer would be accurately reproduced in court, whether by faultless memory or mechanical recording." In the final analysis, the Court concluded, it made no difference if the agent relied on his memory to testify against Lopez or if he used the recording. Just as the agent's memory could be included as evidence at the trial, so could the recording he made.

Justice William Brennan and two other justices issued what have been called "raging" dissents. The Court had erred, Brennan declared, in previous decisions when it failed to bring electronic surveillance under the protection of the Fourth Amendment. Electronic surveillance, he said, was an intolerable invasion of personal privacy and had to be curtailed. Brennan based his argument on a then-recent study by Samuel Dash* entitled *The Eavesdroppers* (1959). A reading of Dash's book, Brennan noted, had shown him that electronic eavesdropping had "become ... pervasively employed by private detectives, police, labor spies, employers, and others."

"These devices," he continued, "... permit a degree of invasion of privacy that can only be described as frightening. Did law enforcement officials have a legitimate need for such widespread use of these devices in their pursuit of criminals?" Brennan asked. He doubted that they did.

Brennan pointed out that there were no studies that showed that criminal investigations would be hindered if there was "a stiff warrant requirement for electronic surveillance." But even without evidence that electronic surveillance devices are necessary for effective police work, he went on, "it must be plain that electronic surveillance imports a peculiarly severe danger to the liberties of the person."

"Electronic surveillance," he concluded, "strikes deeper than at the ancient feeling that a man's home is his castle; it strikes at freedom of communication, a postulate of our kind of society." In modern America, Brennan added, it was simply not enough to protect an individual from traditional searches and seizures; protection also had to be provided to persons against secret recording devices

---

*Samuel Dash is a lawyer who has specialized in legal aspects of electronic surveillance and privacy. During 1973 and 1974, he was chief counsel for the Democrats on the Senate committee that conducted investigations into the Watergate Affair. See page 100.

that "purloin words spoken in confidence within the four walls of home or office."

FROM *KATZ* to NOW

During the 1960s, there began to be signs that the Supreme Court was about to reverse its decision in the famous *Olmstead* case. In the case of *Silverman* v. *United States* (1961), for example, federal agents stuck a "spike mike" into the wall of a suspect's home. The mike was used to transmit conversations that were admitted as evidence to convict the suspect of criminal activity.

In earlier decisions, the Court permitted the use of recording devices when those devices did not physically violate privacy. But in the *Silverman* case, the spike mike made contact with a heating duct and converted, in the Court's words, the Silverman family's "entire heating system into a conductor of sound."

Conversations could be overheard not only in one room, but in every room in the house. In a unanimous decision, the Court declared that Fourth Amendment rights to privacy had been violated. The spike mike, the Court said, had penetrated the Silverman residence and not merely rested on an outside wall. In this case, the warrantless use of a bug was unconstitutional.

Five years later, in the case of *Osborn* v. *United States* (1966), the Court approved of an electronic eavesdropping, but only because it had been carried out under strict judicial supervision. In this case, an undercover agent carried a concealed recorder to tape an attorney's attempt to bribe a juror.

The undercover agent had obtained permission from two federal judges to carry the recorder, after he had reported to authorities several attempts to bribe jurors. The Court upheld the use of the recorder. At issue in this case, it stated, was not permission for the "indiscriminate use" of a listening device. Rather, the issue was "the permissibility of using such a device under the most precise and discriminate circumstances," which the Court declared fully met the requirements of the Fourth Amendment. In *Osborn*, the Court upheld an instance of electronic surveillance because it had been approved, before it had been carried out, by federal judges. Never before had the Court implied that such exacting standards were needed for electronic eavesdropping.

One year after *Osborn*, in the landmark case of *Katz v. United States*, the Supreme Court completely overturned the *Olmstead* decision of thirty-nine years earlier and brought electronic eavesdropping under the protection of the Fourth Amendment. In the *Katz* case, FBI agents placed a listening device and a recorder on the outside wall of a telephone that Katz, a suspected gambler, was known to use.

On the basis of the evidence gathered by the listening device and recorder, Katz was convicted of transmitting wagering information over the telephone. He took his case to the Supreme Court. The FBI, he charged, had had no warrant that permitted the use of the listening device, and therefore had violated his Fourth Amendment rights.

Lawyers for the FBI argued that there had been no need for a warrant. The defendant's Fourth Amendment rights, they claimed, had not been violated because FBI agents had not trespassed on or physically penetrated private property. Furthermore, they pointed out, the telephone booth that Katz used was made largely of glass and had therefore provided no privacy for Katz when he made his call.

The FBI lawyers also noted that the agents had conducted a "very limited search and seizure" that was well within the guidelines that any warrant would have established. The Court, they argued, should uphold the eavesdropping because the FBI had acted with "restraint" and circumspection, and with due regard to Katz's rights.

The Supreme Court, however, disagreed. The "Fourth Amendment," explained Justice Potter Stewart, "protects people, not places." It made no difference, he went on, that the FBI agents had not trespassed on the private property of the suspect, because what they had done in "electronically listening to and recording" Katz's words "violated the privacy upon which he justifiably relied while using the telephone booth. . . ."

When Katz entered the telephone booth, he had every intention and desire for privacy. Stewart explained:

> ...what he sought to exclude when he entered the booth was not the intruding eye—it was the uninvited ear.... One who occupies it, shuts the door behind him, and pays the toll that permits him to place a call, is surely entitled to assume that the words will not be broadcast to the world.

The activities of the FBI agents, Stewart concluded, "in electronically listening to and recording" the defendant's conversation, constituted a violation of the Fourth Amendment's protection against "search and seizure." The Court, he added, believes that a warrant is necessary before a person's privacy can be invaded and that "searches conducted outside the judicial process, without prior approval by judges and magistrates, are per se unreasonable under the Fourth Amendment."

Nor was Stewart persuaded that, because the FBI agents had acted with restraint and circumspection, the eavesdropping should be held constitutional. The "inescapable fact," he noted, "is that this restraint was imposed by the agents themselves, not by a judicial officer. The FBI agents, he stated:

> ...were not required, before commencing the search, to present their estimate of probable cause for detached scrutiny by a neutral magistrate.They were not compelled, during the conduct of the search itself, to observe precise limits established in advance by a specific court order. Nor were they directed, after the search had been completed, to notify the authorizing magistrate in detail of all that had been seized.

Without a warrant and "such safeguards" as a warrant assures, Stewart stated, electronic eavesdropping should not take place. A proper warrant was needed for electronic surveillance, just as it was needed for conventional searches and seizures.

In 1968, the year following the *Katz* decision, Congress undertook to define the legal limits of wiretapping and bugging in the impressively entitled "Omnibus Crime Control and Safe Streets Act." In his state of the union message of 1967, President Lyndon Baines Johnson had urged the passage of a crime control act with strong safeguards for personal privacy. Johnson asked that:

> We should protect what Justice Brandeis called the "right most valued by civilized men"—the right of privacy. We should outlaw all wiretapping—public and private—wherever and whenever it occurs, except when the security of the nation is at stake—and only with the strictest safeguards. We should exercise the full reach of our Constitutional powers to outlaw electronic "bugging" and "snooping."

According to reporters, the section of Johnson's speech that dealt with privacy received more applause from the assembled members of Congress than any of the many other topics he touched upon.

When it passed Congress after long and acrimonious debate, the Omnibus Crime Act made it a crime to wiretap or eavesdrop with an electronic, mechanical, or any other kind of device. The act also made it illegal to procure someone else to wiretap or eavesdrop. Other provisions (1) forbade the disclosure to others of information that was known to have been obtained from wiretaps or bugs; (2) prohibited the manufacture, transportation, or advertisement of devices primarily used to intercept conversations; and (3) excluded from all courts and other government departments, such as legislative and regulatory agencies, all information that was secured in violation of the act.

At first glance, the act seemed to offer strong prohibitions on electronic eavesdropping. But it also listed exceptions to almost every prohibition it announced. The act stated, for example, that "wire or oral communications" can be intercepted where "one of the parties to the communication has given prior consent to such interception." It likewise allowed the president of the United States to sanction wiretaps and bugs in all cases where he judges national security to be at stake.

There were other significant exceptions to the prohibitions on wiretaps and bugs. Once the permission of the United States attorney general had been obtained, the act allowed government agents to use electronic surveillance in cases of major federal felonies. These cases included murder, kidnapping, counterfeiting, narcotics-related crimes, treason, espionage, riots, bribery of public officials, illegal payments to labor unions, and the like. Similarly, state attorneys general, district attorneys, and state judges are permitted to sanction wiretapping and bugging in cases of suspected serious infractions of state laws.

To obtain a warrant to wiretap or eavesdrop, federal or state agents must identify themselves to the proper authority and give "a particular description of the type of communications sought to be intercepted." They must also supply to the authorities "a full and complete statement as to whether or not other investigative procedures have been tried and failed or why they reasonably appear to be unlikely to succeed if tried or to be too dangerous."

The authorities must then carefully weigh the warrant applications and if they choose to grant a warrant, that warrant must follow certain guidelines. A proper warrant must state (1) the name of the person under surveillance and (2) the place that is to be surveyed. It must (3) name the agency or official authorized to carry out the wiretap or bug and (4) give the period of time the eavesdropping is to be in effect.

The Omnibus Crime Act stated that wiretaps or bugs were not to last "for any longer period than is necessary to achieve the objective of the authorization, nor in any event any longer than thirty days." If government agents believe that extensions are needed after thirty days, then they must apply to the proper authorities for new permits. If an individual is wiretapped or bugged, he or she must be informed of the electronic surveillance within ninety days of the issuance of the warrant.

In emergency situations involving national security or organized crime, government agents were permitted to instigate wiretaps or bugs on their own initiative, without a warrant. In such instances, however, the agents must seek judicial approval for the wiretap within forty-eight hours. If judicial authority is not secured within that period, then all evidence obtained as a result of the eavesdropping is inadmissible in court.

Although the Omnibus Crime Act seems an important step in the direction of personal privacy, privacy advocates have had their doubts. They believe that the act permits wiretapping and bugging in far too many instances—from treason and murder to illegal union payments and bribery of government officials. They would prefer to limit electronic surveillance to only the most serious offenses.

But privacy advocates believe the most serious shortcoming of the act is its provision for a thirty-day limit on wiretaps and bugs, a limit that can be extended indefinitely. Thirty days, they argue, is far too long to wiretap a person's telephone or to eavesdrop on private conversations.

Senator Philip Hart (Democrat, Michigan) was one critic of the Omnibus Crime Act. He sat on the Senate Judiciary Committee when that committee considered the Crime Act before it went to the Senate floor for a vote. Hart voted against the act and issued a long statement explaining his opposition to certain of its provisions.

In the course of thirty days, Hart argued, government agents may not only overhear conversations relating to the suspected crime. They might also overhear "irrelevant" and "intimate" conversations between husband and wife, doctor and patient, priest and penitent, and even "constitutionally-privileged" conversations such as those between a lawyer and client. Moreover, Hart noted, all conversations will be overheard "whether they be family, business associates, or visitors...."

"No one," Hart went on, "would suggest that a conventional search warrant may validly be issued to authorize a law enforcement officer to enter a private home or office and embark on a search lasting even a few hours, let alone authorize the officer to move into the premises for a month." Similarly, he stated, "no search warrant could constitutionally authorize all of a person's future written statements to be seized for a thirty-day period, in the hope that one or another of the statements would contain certain incriminating information."

Thirty days, he emphasized in conclusion, was simply too "unlimited" a search into personal privacy. In the *Katz* decision, he pointed out, the Supreme Court had insisted that wiretaps and bugs be covered by the same Fourth Amendment restrictions that govern unreasonable searches and seizures. This meant, he claimed, that wiretaps and bugs could be permitted only under circumstances that were narrowly described and limited in time.

Hart's misgivings were not shared by everyone. In a report issued in January 1972, FBI Director J. Edgar Hoover announced that the wiretapping and bugging powers granted by the Omnibus Crime Act had helped in the "war" against organized crime tremendously. Electronic listening devices, he noted, "have been increasingly valuable in penetrating the complex, tightly knit conspiracies involving intricate security precautions...." Most of the 1,200 arrests recently made in the field of organized crime, he added, were due to the "recent legislation" that allowed increased wiretaps.

THE SUPREME COURT AND NATIONAL SECURITY

The Omnibus Crime Control and Safe Streets Act of 1968 granted wide leeway to the FBI in the use of electronic surveillance against organized crime. The act also attempted to define the powers of the president in dealing with national security emergencies. The act stated that:

> Nothing contained in this statute or in Section 605 of the Communications Act of 1934... shall limit the constitutional powers of the President to take such measures as he deems necessary to protect the Nation against actual or potential attack or to... take such measures as he deems necessary to protect the United States against the overthrow of the government by force or other unlawful means.

The late 1960s and early 1970s were a chaotic and turbulent period in American history. A few extremist New Left groups turned violent and threatened to overturn the American government by force. Anti-Vietnam War demonstrations became massive. Commenting on an anti-war march of 250,000 in Washington, D.C., on November 15, 1969, Attorney General John Mitchell told his wife that the capital city looked like what Russia must have looked like during the early days of the Russian Revolution.

Reacting to the rising tide of violent anti-war and leftist protest, the Nixon administration declared that it interpreted the Omnibus Crime Act as permitting the president to instigate wiretaps and electronic eavesdropping in the present troublesome circumstances that the nation faced. Attorney General John Mitchell stated that "the president, acting through the attorney general, may constitutionally authorize the use of electronic surveillance in cases where it was determined, that in order to preserve the national security, the use of such surveillance is reasonable." This, he concluded, was the president's "inherent power."

In an attempt to bring New Left and anti-war movements under control, government agents infiltrated extremist organizations they regarded as "subversive" and used electronic surveillance to keep track of their activities. In one important instance, leftists charged with conspiracy to destroy government property took their case to the Supreme Court, arguing that the government had violated their privacy by warrantless taps on their telephones.

In the case of *United States* v. *United States District Court, Eastern Michigan* (1972), the government admitted that wiretaps had been used to gather evidence against the "radicals" and that no warrants had been issued permitting those wiretaps. The government claimed, however, that the taps had been approved by the attorney general of the United States as part of an investigation of dangerous and subversive organizations.

Wiretapping, the government lawyers explained, was an essential element in the Nixon administration's program to maintain the security of the United States against those who sought to destroy it. Because the wiretaps involved something so serious as national security, they added, the government should not be required to obtain a proper warrant every time a wiretap was needed. Moreover, they went on, the case at hand was extremely serious because the wiretaps had uncovered leftists intent on bombing buildings where military research was being carried out.

In an 8 to 0 decision, however, the Supreme Court rejected the government's argument. Justice Lewis Powell wrote the decision for the Court. He noted that among Americans there was a "deep-seated uneasiness and apprehension" that electronic surveillance techniques such as wiretapping would be used "to intrude upon cherished privacy of law-abiding citizens." This uneasiness, Powell went on, led him to conclude that government officials responsible for the investigation and prosecution of crime should not be the sole judges of when "a constitutionally sensitive" act, such as wiretapping, should be used.

Why should government officials not be trusted to have the sole responsibility to determine if wiretaps could be used? Government officials, Powell pointed out, "may yield too readily to pressures to obtain incriminating evidence and overlook potential invasion of privacy and protected speech," which are guaranteed by a "convergence" of First and Fourth Amendment rights. It was the responsibility of the Court, he emphasized, to defend citizens from overzealous law officers who would overlook constitutional rights in their vigorous pursuit of evidence.

Moreover, Powell continued, all forms of surveillance run the risk of violating constitutional rights no matter what their ultimate purposes might be. The infringement of rights takes place, he believed, whether the surveillance is part of a criminal investigation or part of an "on-going intelligence gathering" mission. In either case, the government may have acted to undermine basic and fundamental rights.

Powell believed that electronic surveillance violated the right to speak in dissent of government policies. It has been abundantly shown, he pointed out, that a government tends "to view with suspicion those who most fervently dispute its policies." It has also been shown, he noted, that governments will resort to various methods to help silence and destroy dissent.

In this case, Powell stated, the government has defended its illegal wiretaps on the basis of a need to protect the "national security." For Powell, this defense was "vague" and unacceptable. Private dissent, he argued, "no less than public discourse is essential to our free society."

It should not be sacrificed to an amorphous concept like "national security."

The Supreme Court, he concluded, believes that lawful private dissent is protected by the Constitution. Those who dissent lawfully should not be subjected to the "dread" of "an unchecked surveillance power" that invades their privacy. Nor should "the fear of unauthorized official eavesdropping," he added, be allowed to "deter vigorous citizen dissent and discussion of Government action in private conversations."

In the historic *Katz* decision, the Supreme Court brought electronic eavesdropping under the privacy protections of the Fourth Amendment. In the Omnibus Crime Act of 1968, Congress set legal limitations on the use of wiretaps and bugs. In the *U.S.* v. *U.S. District Court* case, the Court declared that the president could not use "national security" as an excuse to wiretap without proper warrants.

Have these high court decisions and congressional statutes brought illegal electronic surveillance under control? Privacy experts say that they have not. Illegal wiretapping and bugging, they claim, continue to be widespread both in government and in the private sector.

In the mid-1970s, a series of scandals and revelations uncovered illegal electronic eavesdropping in the highest quarters of government. In June 1972, in the midst of a presidential election, burglars were discovered inside the Democratic National Headquarters in the Watergate in Washington, D.C. The investigations that followed in 1973 and 1974 into the so-called "Watergate Affair" showed that the burglars were in the Watergate to install wiretaps on telephones, and that they had been hired by men who worked at the White House. The investigations also revealed that White House aides had ordered illegal wiretaps of the telephones of leading journalists and high government officials distrusted by the Nixon administration; that they had arranged the burglary of the offices of a Los Angeles psychiatrist in order to obtain confidential information on one of his patients; and that they had performed other acts that violated the privacy of American citizens.

Numerous privacy violations were also discovered by Senate and presidential committee investigations into the activities of the FBI and CIA in 1974 and 1975. Among other things, it was found that the FBI had conducted a campaign of harassment against "radicals" it regarded as dangerous to American security, including actress Jane Fonda and civil rights leader Dr. Martin Luther King, Jr.

The campaign of harassment included the wiretapping of Dr. King's telephones, with the approval of Attorney General Robert Kennedy but without proper judicial warrant, and other acts of electronic eavesdropping. The investigations also revealed that the CIA had opened the mail of private citizens over a period of more than a decade and had kept illegal files on thousands of American "subversives"—in direct violation of the CIA charter, which forbids CIA activity within the United States.

There are no accurate and trustworthy reports on how widespread electronic eavesdropping is in the private, nongovernmental sections of society. However, privacy experts say that there is no reason to believe that it is any less prevalent there than in the government. The only way to deal effectively with wiretapping and bugging, the experts tell us, is through forceful legislation that limits the manufacture and sale of electronic listening devices. But the Congress, they point out, has avoided this course of action.

Privacy experts are also concerned about another form of electronic and mechanical surveillance that neither Congress nor the courts have faced. Lawyer Stephen Gillers, author of *Getting Justice* (1973), points out that infrared cameras can now take pictures in total darkness. Telescopic lenses can focus on and take pictures of the activities of people when they are in their own homes. Yet the law has not addressed these forms of the invasion of privacy.

In his 1968 statement to Congress deploring the inadequacies of the Omnibus Crime Act, Senator Philip Hart outlined the problems that face us in protecting privacy from electronic and mechanical surveillance. "In yesteryear," Hart said, "a man could retire into his home or office free from the prying eye or ear." But now, he continued:

That time is...long past. Transmitting microphones the size of a sugar cube can be bought for less than $10. Other gadgets now enable a would-be snooper in New York to eavesdrop in Los Angeles merely by dialing a telephone number....

Directional microphones of the "shotgun" and parabolic mike type make it possible, by aiming the mike at a subject, to overhear conversations several hundred feet away. Laser beams permit an eavesdropper to monitor conversations in rooms up to half a mile away by aiming the beam at a thin wall or window. And the experts now tell us that in the years to come, as the methods of eavesdropping technology surge forward, the problems of protecting personal privacy will even further intensify.

Clearly, Hart concluded, personal privacy in America is under serious threat and unless more efforts are made to safeguard privacy rights, it will not be long before "individual privacy will shrink to the vanishing point."

8
THE INFORMATION GATHERERS: PERSONALITY TESTS AND POLYGRAPHS

Privacy is the right to control your own living space, as in the right to be free from unreasonable searches and seizures. Privacy is the right to control your own identity, as in the right to be known by a name of your choice and not a number, the right to choose your own hair and dress styles, the right to personality. Privacy is the right to control information about yourself, as in the right to prevent disclosure of private facts and the right to know which information is kept and how it is used.

Robert Ellis Smith,
Privacy: How to Protect What's Left of It (1980)

en and women in search of work may come to the conclusion that they have no privacy left at all. Employers ask many questions. They ask for a person's name, address, marital status, and social security number.* They are also likely to request data on previous employment, arrest record, military background, and education, and to require a new employee to fill out tax forms and forms relating to medical and insurance benefits.

All this information goes into an employee's personal file and is stored away on computer or elsewhere. In addition, an employer may ask an employee to submit to a "personality test" or a polygraph test designed to reveal even more about the employee's character and habits. Or an employer may hire private investigators to look into an employee's background, question his or her friends and relatives, and collect further data. All this information, too, is stored in the employee's file.

How much information is an employer entitled to? A Louis Harris poll showed that most American employees believed that it was reasonable for employers to ask questions about pregnancy, alcoholism, and drug abuse. But the poll also revealed that the same employees believed they had been asked to turn over too much private information to their employers. Between 76 and 92 percent of the employees interviewed said that questions about friends, neighborhood, spouse, arrest record, and political affiliation were excessive and improper. A majority also found questions about psychiatric counseling, credit status, and home ownership excessive. Fifty percent of the

*When Social Security numbers were first put into use in the 1930s, they were regarded as private and confidential. Today the numbers are so frequently used to identify an individual that some privacy experts have wondered if future Americans will more often be known by their numbers than they are by their names.

employees thought that psychological testing by employers should be "forbidden by law."

This chapter will look at two of the methods employers use to find out information about employees: personality tests and polygraph tests. Two questions will be asked. First, do these kinds of tests intrude unfairly into a person's privacy? And second, if they do, what can be done to protect an individual's privacy when these tests are used?

PERSONALITY TESTING

To test a job applicant's "personality" and "aptitude," many employers hire the services of professional testing organizations. The tests administered by these organizations are usually variations on the Minnesota Multiphasic Personality Inventory and were developed to reveal the strengths and weaknesses of a person's character.

One such test is the Emotional Stability test, or ES. The ES asks personal questions from which a judgment of the applicant's "stability" and "maturity" is made. Among many others, the ES asks the following questions:

> Were you a bed wetter between the ages of 8 to
>   14 years?
> Do you feel you are as good as most people?
> Do you always sweat and get tied up in knots
>   during examinations?

Another frequently used personality test is the Trustworthiness Attitude test, or TA. The TA asks questions like the following, requiring a "yes" or "no" response from the person being tested:

> A lot of employees steal because they are not
>   satisfied with their job.
> Breaking the law can sometimes be justifiable.
> Society actually encourages rebelliousness by
>   having too many rules.

An employee's response to these questions, according to the makers of the test, can determine his or her level of "trustworthiness."

Another personality test that has been used by the federal government to test new government employees asks the tested person to respond with "true" or "false" to these questions:

> I feel sure there is only one true religion.
> My sex life is satisfactory.
> During one period when I was a youngster I engaged in petty thievery.
> I believe there is a God.
> Once in a while I laugh at a dirty joke.

Another test used by the federal government asked the tested person to "choose the one most applicable to you" among pairs of statements like the following:

> A. I feel like blaming others when things go wrong for me.
> B. I feel I am inferior in most respects.
>
> A. I like to listen to or tell jokes in which sex plays a major part.
> B. I feel like getting revenge when someone has insulted me.

Note that the tested person cannot reject both statements as false, but must choose one of the two as more nearly describing his or her own personality.

Clearly, the questions listed above are deeply personal questions and require an individual to be open about habits and beliefs once regarded as completely private and confidential. Are employers justified in requiring employees to take these tests? Many experts claim that they are.

The director of J. N. Farr Associates, a testing service, has written that the tests do not constitute a violation of privacy, because every question asked is job-related. Some jobs, he pointed out, require "aggressiveness" on the part of an employee. Wasn't it reasonable, he continued, to expect an employer to want a potential employee tested to see if he or she were aggressive enough to handle the job? It is qualities like aggressiveness, he concluded, that the tests are specifically designed to discover.

—— 107

Case and Co., another testing service, has justified its work by asking "What would happen if personality tests were not used?" The answer, they concluded, was "that the judgments that are made about people without tests may be more biased and harmful than the judgments that are made with the use of them." It is better to trust the "objectivity" of a test than to rely on the possible prejudice of an individual interviewer.

Many experts, however, believe that personality tests are inadequate and unscientific. The noted psychiatrist Dr. Karl Menninger, for instance, has said that most personality tests are "not worth the paper they're printed on."

The problem with personality tests, the critics say, is that they ask too much personal information and that they are not reliable. Intelligent people, they point out, can learn to manipulate their answers in order to achieve the effect desired by the test—and therefore reveal nothing true about themselves. But a person of good character, who fears taking tests, may perform awkwardly and poorly.

There is no reason to believe, the critics conclude, that a person who reveals the quality of "aggressiveness" or "honesty" on a test will display these qualities on the job. What personality tests actually test, they add, is the ability to take a test—and nothing more. Meanwhile, they note, the tests have ferreted information out of an individual, information that should remain private and confidential.

After a close analysis of personality testing, Dr. Karl U. Smith, professor of industrial psychology at the University of Wisconsin, came to some strong conclusions about the tests. He presented his findings to a congressional committee concerned with privacy.

1) Psychological testing has no critical relations with experimental psychology or any other branch of experimental science and reflects none of the recent advances in scientific understanding of mechanisms of behavior; 2) testing is based largely on estimating deviations from social norms and has no significant means within itself of dealing with the individual; and 3) there are no objective scientific principles to guide test construction.

As a result of Dr. Smith's findings and of other evidence critical of personality testing, Rep. Cornelius Gallagher (Democrat, New Jersey), chairman of the House Special Subcommittee on Invasion of Privacy, denounced personality testing from the House floor in 1965. Personality testing, Gallagher said, was "a gross invasion of privacy into the lives and thoughts of our public workers...an insidious invasion of privacy and illegal search of the human mind."

Gallagher's subcommittee made several recommendations that led to a review of many personality testing practices in the federal government. Since that time many private employers have also reviewed personality testing and made changes in policy. Legislation and the courts, however, have provided no protection against the invasion of privacy presented by personality tests, and the tests remain in frequent use today.

THE POLYGRAPH

According to various estimates, between 250 thousand and 2 million polygraph examinations—also called "lie-detector" tests—are administered each year in the United States. About 80 percent of these tests are given by firms that specialize in polygraph testing and are hired by employers to check on the honesty of potential or current employees. Among the most frequent users of polygraph testing services are supermarket and drug store chains, the beer-brewing company Coors, McDonald's, and Burger Chef.

According to a brochure published by a leading polygraphy company, about 30 percent of any group of potential employees can be expected to be "undesirable" for one reason or another—and lie detector tests will uncover this 30 percent. Privacy experts, however, point out that there are no accurate figures on how many job applicants fail the tests because the polygraph detects that they possess undesirable traits, or how many are not hired simply because of "admissions" or "confessions" they made about themselves in the course of the test.

"The main victims" of polygraphs, privacy expert Robert Ellis Smith has stated, "are youngsters entering the job market for the first time, often to be paid at the minimum wage or below it. They are nervous about beginning work and distrustful of many employers." Their nervousness, he concludes, makes it difficult for them to be tested with any degree of accuracy or fairness.

What is a polygraph? It is an electronic device developed shortly after World War I to measure breathing patterns, blood pressure, and skin resistance to external current (called galvanic skin response). Breathing is measured by a rubber tube placed around the individual's chest. Blood pressure is measured by a cuff around the arm. Electrodes attached to the fingers measure the galvanic skin response.

The polygraph machine records each of these responses on paper. Polygraph testers assume that if a person lies in response to a question, his or her body will show stress or tension in reaction to the lie. The testers also assume that this stress and tension will reveal itself in changes in blood pressure, respiration, and galvanic skin response, which, in turn, will be detected by the polygraph machine. Truthful answers, on the other hand, will result in no significant stress or tension and will give the machine little or nothing to detect.

Like personality tests, the polygraph examination is designed to weed out employees who are dishonest and untrustworthy. According to polygraph testers, the average test should last about two hours. But privacy experts claim that many polygraph tests are done in assembly-line fashion in a short amount of time, particularly when a large number of potential employees are to be tested. When the subject of the test is an employee on the job whose veracity is in question, then more time and care are taken in the examination.

At the beginning of the test, the examiner asks the person being tested innocuous questions to establish the person's basic breathing, skin, and blood pressure reactions. Other questions about theft, dishonesty, alcoholism, and the like will follow.

Defenders of polygraph tests argue that they are scientifically accurate and correct at least 90 percent of the time, if not more. If a person has nothing to hide, they say, he or she should not fear the lie-detector because the machine provides an impartial means to separate the honest from the dishonest.

The critics of polygraphs, however, believe otherwise. David Lykken, a University of Minnesota psychologist, estimated that the accuracy of polygraph tests is somewhere between 64 and 72 percent. This is low, he pointed out, because a simple flip of the coin could achieve 50 percent accuracy. In an article that appeared in the March 1975 issue of *Psychology Today*, Lykken argued that even if polygraph tests achieved a 90 percent accuracy, they would still be undesirable. "If we assume that the test is valid 90 percent of the time," he wrote, "the mathematics of the situation go something like this."

Imagine a company of 1,000 employees, 50 of whom are "pilferers." A lie-detector will uncover forty-five of the fifty, or 90 percent of the pilferers, but let five go free. It will also detect 855 of the 950 honest employees and judge them correctly as innocent. But the remaining ninety-five honest workers will fail the test and be assumed to be guilty. This means, Lykken concluded, that more than 2 out of 3 of the 140 employees who fail the test will be innocent, but will lose their jobs. "It is plain," he added, "that too many innocent persons suffer when lie-detector tests are used to screen employees."

Since 1970 two new devices, similar to the polygraph, have been in use: Voice Analyzers and psychological stress evaluators, or PSEs. Both devices are designed to record changes in stress in the human voice, giving indication of dishonesty. Experts have determined that the Voice Analyzer has an accuracy rate of 32 percent, or less than pure chance. The U.S. Army Land Warfare Laboratory estimated that the accuracy of the PSE was between 19 and 33 percent. Defenders of both machines, however, ardently argue for their use in crime detection.

INSTANCES OF
POLYGRAPH FAILURE
Critics of polygraph tests are fond of pointing to instances when the tests have failed:

☐   In Los Angeles, a lie-detector test was given to a female employee of a supermarket. "Did you check out items to your mother on a discount?" she was asked. The polygraph machine registered stress and the examiner decided that her response to the question was "deceptive." The employee was fired. Only later, it was discovered that her response to the inquiry about her mother had resulted because her mother was dead and the employee was reacting to the thought of her mother's death.

☐ Tom Hemmert of Lima, Ohio, worked for Allied Food Mart. One summer, a shortage of $1,000 was found in the store where he worked, and all employees were asked to take lie-detector tests. Hemmert willingly agreed to take the test. One of the questions he was asked was "Do you know who took the money?" Hemmert had suspicions about who had stolen the money, but he didn't know for sure. The polygraph machine, however, detected a fluctuation in his body's response to the question and the examiner assumed that he had something to hide. The examiner informed Allied Food, and Hemmert was dismissed. His labor union took up his case and managed to get him reinstated.

☐ In Joan Barthel's excellent book, *Death in Canaan* (1976), another instance of polygraph error is vividly described. One evening, Peter Reilly, an eighteen-year-old who lived with his mother in a small house near Canaan, Connecticut, returned home to find his mother brutally murdered. That night and into the next day, police questioned him intensely, allowing him little rest and little to eat.

Reilly agreed to a polygraph test. Barthel shows in detail how his tiredness and his belief in the scientific accuracy of the test led Reilly to be convinced that he had committed the murder in a moment of insanity that he could not recall. Assured by the polygraph examiner that he was holding something back and not telling the truth, Reilly denied the validity of his own memory—which told him that he had not committed the crime—and assumed that the machine could sense what he had done better than he could. He "confessed" to the murder.

As friends and neighbors in the Canaan community came to realize what had happened, they took up his cause. But it took years of strenuous effort on their part before they were able to arrange for a new trial and secure his release.

☐ Polygraphs not only can be wrong, the critics say, they can also be used for unsavory purposes. Consider the story of Don M. Blews, told in 1978 to a congressional hearing on lie-detector tests. Between 1973 and 1978, he said, he had been a store manager for a department store chain that had 106 stores in four southern states.

Blews said that two months after he had begun to manage his third store for the company, his district supervisor arrived and noticed that there were two black women working there. Blews was told to fire the women, "because the company had a policy against hiring blacks." When he refused, Blews was told by the supervisor, "OK, Mr. Blews, we'll have to show you how our polygraph test works around here."

Two days later, a polygraph examiner arrived and tested every employee in the store, including Mr. Blews. When he left, the examiner told Blews that only two employees had failed the examination—the two black women. Their polygraph printouts, the examiner said, had shown "a sign of a possibility of deceit."

But on two previous occasions, the two black women had passed polygraph tests administered by the same polygraph testing company. Clearly, Blews believed, the tests had been used to weed them out because they were black.

THE CASE AGAINST
POLYGRAPHS
The House of Representatives Committee on Government Operations concluded in 1965 that "there is no 'lie detector,' neither machine nor human. People have been deceived by a myth that a metal box in the hands of an investigator can detect truth and falsehood."

—— 113

Ten years later, in 1976, the same committee once again investigated polygraphs and came to the same conclusion. "The clear import of the hearing on which this report is based," the committee concluded, "leads to the same conclusion as was reached in 1965." The committee recommended that polygraph examinations be eliminated from use by employers.

Why are so many experts critical of polygraphs? William H. Winn of the Retail Clerks Union believes that polygraphs are a "gratuitous insult to human dignity." They allow employers to harass and intimidate employees, he points out, and to keep them in line.

Andrew Kahn of the AFL-CIO has noted the basic unfairness of polygraphs. They discriminate against the powerless and the lowly. "Bank tellers take polygraph tests; bank presidents do not," he has stated. "Grocery clerks take polygraph tests; most store managers do not." Clearly, he has concluded, whether you will take a polygraph test or not depends largely on your level of income and the class you belong to.

Critics also regard polygraph tests as an assault on basic privacy rights. In a lie-detector examination, says John Shattuck of the American Civil Liberties Union, "no subject is beyond the pale. Once hooked to the machine, the person must answer any question; if he hedges or denies, he will be accused of deception."

Moreover, the information an individual reveals during a polygraph test may become part of his or her permanent record. "There is every likelihood," noted former Senator Sam Ervin, a strong privacy advocate, "that a record of the employee's responses may find its way into the personnel files of the company or agency and be transmitted as 'reference material' when the worker leaves, despite assurances to the contrary."

Critics believe that polygraph testing may violate constitutional protections. American courts, they point out, almost never allow the admission of polygraph evidence in a trial. If the courts refuse to consider this material, they ask, why then should employers be allowed to accept it? Critics also believe that the polygraph may violate Fourth Amendment rights. Polygraph examiners, they note, ask deeply probing questions that uncover an individual's innermost beliefs. Is not this, they ask, an unreasonable search and seizure of a person's valued possessions?

The critics also see possible Fifth Amendment violations in the use of polygraphs. An employee who refuses to take a lie-detector test, they argue, may discover that he or she is assumed to be hiding something. On the other hand, if the person submits to the test, he or she may be compelled to reveal damaging and incriminating evidence—an infringement of the right "to remain silent" and not testify against oneself.

The polygraph may likewise be in violation of the Sixth Amendment, critics say. The Sixth Amendment guarantees that "In all criminal prosecutions, the accused shall enjoy the right . . . to be confronted with the witnesses against him." But as Sam Ervin has pointed out, "it's hard to cross-examine a machine."

The critics call the whole theory behind polygraph testing into question. Polygraph examinations "work," says Andrew Kahn, only because people are led to believe they work. "By leaving favorable literature around the testing area, wearing clinical garb, and using scientific jargon," Kahn explains, the examiner attempts to produce an aura of scientific exactness that the tests simply don't have.

Moreover, the critics add, many people are psychologically and temperamentally unsuited to taking polygraph tests, and pathological liars can fool the machine. "What is recorded," Senator Ervin has noted, "is not the subject's veracity, but his physiological responses to an examiner's questions." It is the examiner's interpretation of the data on the machine, he explained, "and not some demonstrated physical fact that determines the truthfulness of the individual's response."

Senate hearings on polygraphs in 1977 and 1978 showed that lie-detector tests produce fear among many who have nothing to hide, but who simply fear examinations and tests. "There is a difference," said Senator Birch Bayh (Democrat, Indiana), "between someone who has nothing to hide . . . and someone who may not want to disclose everything in his or her background to a public forum or to a polygraph interrogator." Yet the polygraph cannot distinguish between the two, and interprets both as "deceptive."

—— 115

Finally, critics fear that the so-called "polygraph experts" who administer the tests and interpret them are not experts at all. Polygraph "experts," they point out, receive only about six weeks of training in the use of the polygraph machine. Investigation has shown that most of them do not have any educational background that would qualify them as experts on human behavior. Indeed, less than 1 percent of polygraph examiners today have had training in psychology.

William Petrocelli has written that regulations governing polygraph examiners are weak. In a majority of states, he notes, there are no requirements at all for polygraph interrogators and, says Petrocelli, anyone who purchases a polygraph machine can "go into business immediately."

PROTECTIONS AGAINST POLYGRAPHS

As a result of Senate hearings on privacy in 1977 and 1978, Senator Birch Bayh introduced a bill designed to limit the use of polygraphs. Support for the bill was strong from the American Civil Liberties Union and from labor unions seeking to protect their members from polygraph testing.

Opposition to the bill, however, was intense. Employers claimed that lie-detecting devices were essential to uncover dishonest employees. Law enforcement officials spoke of the polygraph's role in crime detection. The bill failed to pass.

Some protection against polygraphs has come from elsewhere. Five states now prohibit employers from requesting that employees take polygraph tests. Eleven other states prohibit the administration of required tests, but allow employers to administer optional polygraph examinations.

Polygraph critics, however, believe that optional tests are a mixed blessing. They allow a person to refuse to take a polygraph test, but they offer no protection from employers who reject potential employees simply because they refuse to take the test. A person who exercises his or her freedom to turn down the test may find that the job is no longer open—and yet have no way to challenge the employer's rejection.

Moreover, the critics add, neither the federal government nor any state has passed regulations that control the use of the data collected during polygraph examinations. The admissions and statements a person makes during the test may find their way into the records of the polygraph company, the employer, or elsewhere where they can be found and used by later investigators.

Most successful opposition to polygraph examinations has come from labor unions. Some unions have successfully negotiated contracts with employers that prohibit the use of polygraph tests. Others have approached the problem on a case by case basis, working for the reinstatement of employees who have lost their jobs unjustly because of polygraphs.

In the absence of adequate legal protection, polygraph critics recommend that the best way to avoid a lie-detector test is to refuse all jobs that require such a test. But if you find you must take the test, the critics suggest three measures: (1) ask what the credentials of the person administering the test are; and (2) find out what the results of the test are, along with an explanation of the results.

But most important, (3) discover whether or not the employer offers the opportunity of appeal within the company. If your results are negative, you may have the right to challenge them and appeal your case. You may find, too, that you have the right to add a qualifying explanation to your file or to see that the test results are not made a part of your permanent record.

9
THE INFORMATION GATHERERS: PRIVACY IN THE COMPUTER AGE

Privacy is necessary to the development of a free and independent people. To preserve this privacy, our national lethargy and lack of knowledge must be countered.... People must be made to realize that, little by little, they are losing their right to privacy. Once they become aware of this, I think they will shake off their apathy and demand action. Then, and only then, will we get strong legislation to protect a reasonable amount of our right to be left alone.

Senator Edward Long
of Missouri, *The Intruders:
The Invasion of Privacy
by Government and
Industry* (1966)

odern America has become a nation of record-keepers. According to Marc Uri Porat, author of *The Information Economy* (1977), more than half of all labor income in the United States now comes from the production, processing, and distribution of information. Thanks to modern technology most of this information is now stored in computers and data banks, from where it can be almost instantly retrieved.

A July 12, 1982 article in *U.S. News & World Report* entitled "Report on Privacy: Who is Watching You?" estimated that the various agencies of the federal government have a grand total of more than three and one-half billion files on American citizens—an average of fifteen files for each American. Many additional files are kept by state and local governments.

The *U.S. News & World Report* article also pointed to the large amount of data held by private businesses on American citizens. Each year, credit bureaus compile more than twenty-five million reports on American consumers. Schools and colleges maintain records on the academic performances of students. There are also millions of medical files, insurance forms, and banking records that hold private and confidential material.

There seems to be no end to modern society's thirst for information, and computers now make possible the storage of more information than ever before. Computer experts predict that we shall shortly have the capacity to match, link, and exchange all sorts of data now in separate computer banks—through electronic means. This means that all the information now in a variety of government and private computers can be pulled together, at a moment's notice, to form a complete dossier on each American citizen.

Privacy advocates take a dim view of our computerized future. They fear that computers present a dangerous threat to basic American liberties. "We are stumbling into an electronic future without any sense of whether anyone's privacy will be protected," William Petrocelli has written.

This chapter will look at the fears that privacy advocates have about computers and at what steps have been taken to help ensure personal privacy in the computer age.

COMPUTERS AND PRIVACY

Privacy advocates see two general threats to basic American values in a computerized society. First, they believe that a computerized society will lead to an erosion of individual autonomy and freedom of choice. Second, they point out that the information stored in computers is subject to theft and misuse.

Computers challenge individual autonomy, the privacy advocates say, because one of the results of their use is increased social control. The collection of enormous amounts of personal and confidential information, they note, is to reward those people who have "good" records and weed out those who have "undesirable" ones.

But is this fair? the privacy advocates ask. Should a person's past record be used to determine his or her future behavior? Should a file become permanent and universally available, forever branding a person according to its contents? Representative Cornelius Gallagher, chairman of a House committee looking into threats to privacy, voiced this concern when he said:

> It is our greatest fear that modern computer technology will attempt to do just that—to establish on the basis of compiled data on man's past actions axiomatic principles for predicting what he will do in the future—and that these principles will become accepted by society as nearly infallible. The final result would be the restriction of a man's future based upon the statistical pattern of his actions in his youth.... We are now on the brink of making a fundamental change in our society which will destroy the basic philosophy of letting a man start anew, his record unblemished by past mistakes.... America appears to be moving slowly but steadily toward a doctrine of complete scientific objectivity which will categorize and catalog each aspect of individuality, leaving as an end result a stack of computer program cards where once were human beings.

Social critic Vance Packard has stated similar fears about computers. "'Big Brother,' if he ever comes to the United States," Packard warned, "may turn out to be not a greedy power-seeker, but rather a relentless bureaucrat obsessed with efficiency. And he, more than the simple power-seeker, could lead us to that ultimate of horrors, a humanity in chains of plastic tape" fed into computers.

For the sake of human autonomy and freedom, the privacy advocates say, a computerized future must be avoided. Because computers can be used as a tool to control and manipulate, they are at odds with democracy's emphasis on the importance of individual decision making and private opinion. A free society cannot be one that relies on machines to form its memory and make its decisions.

Privacy advocates believe that computers challenge American society at its roots. On the one hand, America can move toward computerization and all that it entails: complete order and efficiency and loss of individual autonomy. Or America can reassert its traditional values and establish areas where individual choice and freedom can be asserted, free of the authority of computerized information.

The second general area of complaint voiced by the privacy advocates is the fallibility of computers. Information put into computers, they claim, is often unverified, inaccurate, incomplete, and subject to misinterpretation— yet because this data has been computerized, it is regarded as "scientific" and "objective."

No one has written more tellingly and clearly on computers and privacy than Arthur Miller, a professor at the University of Michigan Law School. Although his book *The Assault on Privacy* (1971) was written more than ten years ago, its concerns about computers still stand today.

"In a typical remote-access time-sharing system,"* Miller pointed out, "there are at least six points through which distortion of the information may occur." The first is the information itself. The data must be "translated"

---

*A remote-access time-sharing system is a computer that has several users, each with his or her own set of information, and that also has terminals at other locations, perhaps hundreds of miles away.

into the language of the machine, and is therefore subject to the intrusion of the translator. Furthermore, once the data is "machine-readable," it is stored on punch cards, magnetic tapes, discs, data cells and the like—all of which are subject to theft or duplication.

The second vulnerable point occurs when the information is moved from the files into the central processor. Computers are intricate and delicate machines, and capable of a number of malfunctions. "Thus," Miller wrote, "a minor mechanical flaw or variations in electric current— let alone a power failure—can result in data being lost, distorted, or misdirected to an unauthorized recipient...."

At this stage, too, a computer user may be able to pick up a "residuum" of information left in the computer by the previous user. Or an eavesdropper could capture the electromagnetic signals radiating from the computer, and have them reconstructed elsewhere—thus gaining access to the information the computer is processing.

Furthermore, the codes used to prevent access to information stored in the computer are not difficult to break. Experts believe that a computer programmer with only a high school diploma could break complex protective codes in five hours or less. For a person with greater computer expertise, the time would be shorter. "Thus," Professor Miller noted, "it is rather distressing that many academic, commercial, and industrial time-share data systems containing personal information have little or nothing in the way of access controls protecting their files."

The third vulnerable point is the personnel who service the computer. Like all humans, they are subject to bribery or other forms of persuasion. A programmer, for instance, could program the machine so that data fall into unauthorized hands, or the programmer could arrange to have an unauthorized party gain access to the machine to collect data.

The fourth vulnerable point comes when information is sent from the central processor through communication links. At this stage, transmission lines can be tapped and the electronic communication passing over them can be recorded. Or wiretappers could attach their own computer terminal to the line, allowing them, Miller wrote, "to gain entry to all the time-share customers' files."

The fifth and sixth points of vulnerability are the switching center and the remote-access terminals. At both of these points, the computer is subject to eavesdropping. A computer expert can tamper with the switching center, causing information to flow to an undesignated source. Moreover, Miller added, since remote-access terminals can be located anywhere in the world, it is "virtually impossible for any individual to police the flow of information about him."

With computers so vulnerable, Miller concluded, we can expect "elements of organized crime, a variety of governmental agencies (especially the law enforcement establishment), and segments of private industry" to take advantage of that vulnerability. There is simply too much valuable information stored in computers, he added, for us to expect them to remain safe from probes by unauthorized parties.

Professor Miller also had something to say about the accuracy of computers. "A large corporate or welfare databank," he noted, "may contain information on a person's education, military record, medical history, employment background, aptitude and psychological testing performance, as well as a number of subjective appraisals of his character and skills."

"Any of this information," he continued, "might be entirely accurate and sufficient when viewed from one perspective but be wholly incomplete and misleading when viewed from another." Take, for example, a computer printout that describes a man as a "convicted felon." No mention is made of the nature of his crime. It might be armed robbery. It might be an arrest during a civil rights demonstration in the 1960s. But in either case, the individual is branded undesirable.

Miller feared that a person's computer file—assumed to be scientifically precise—would become nothing more than a "hearsay narrative," filled with misleading information that follows them from cradle to grave. This prospect, he said, is "made even more depressing by the realization that much of the increased bulk of the data likely to find their way into the files will be gathered and processed by relatively unskilled and unimaginative people who will lack the discrimination...necessary to justify reliance on their judgment."

COMPUTERS AND PRIVACY:
THE RECORD OF
THE FEDERAL GOVERNMENT
Since 1970, the federal government has conducted investigations and passed laws concerning privacy and computers. Privacy advocates, however, have been highly critical of these efforts and believe that much more must be done before individual privacy is adequately protected against intrusion by computer technology.

What follows is a discussion of the legislation passed by Congress and other measures taken by the government that deal with computers and privacy.

The Fair Credit Reporting Act of 1970 (FCRA). Congress directed the FCRA against credit reporting agencies and designed the act to correct abuses and misuses of consumer credit information. Credit reporting agencies investigate credit records. They also do background checks on employment and insurance records. The amount of data they gather on an individual can be enormous.

Among the provisions of the FCRA were the following:

(1) The act prohibits the reporting of "obsolete information" more than seven years old, except for bankruptcies, for which the limit is fourteen years.

(2) The act also restricts credit reporting agencies from taking information from an earlier report and using it in a later report unless the old information is "verified in the process of making such subsequent consumer report."

(3) The act requires that a person ordering a check by a credit reporting agency must inform a con-

sumer in writing, "not later than three days after the date on which the report was first requested," that a consumer investigation is being conducted on him or her. If the consumer requests further information, the agency must make "a complete and accurate disclosure of the nature and the scope of the investigation."

(4) The FCRA requires the credit reporting agency to disclose "the nature and substance of all information in its files" if a consumer requests that information.

(5) The act likewise allows the consumer to find out the reasons behind any denial of credit, employment, or insurance that he or she may experience as a result of a consumer report. If the consumer is dissatisfied with the "completeness or accuracy" of the report, the agency must reinvestigate the item in question. And, finally, if the consumer is still dissatisfied after the reinvestigation, he or she may attach to the report a short personal statement—of one hundred words or less—explaining his or her side of the disputed information.

Privacy advocates believe that these provisions might have gone a long way toward correcting abuses of private information by credit reporting agencies—if Congress had written a stronger bill. As it stands, the critics say, the FCRA is so full of exceptions and loopholes that it provides next to no protection at all.

Critics point out that the act provides no penalty for the disclosure of incorrect or obsolete information. All that a credit reporting agency must do is show that it has established "reasonable procedures" to avoid disclosure of such material.

Furthermore, the critics add, the act does not really require agencies to turn all the information in their files over to a person who requests it. The act requires that the agency supply only a *summary* of the data that is in a person's credit record.

A major loophole in the act, the critics explain, is that it is directed only against the handling of information by credit reporting agencies. Other agencies or persons are not included. Thus an individual not connected with a credit agency can obtain another person's credit record and not be bound by the restrictions of the FCRA.

The Privacy Act of 1974. Section 2 of the Privacy Act of 1974 states that "the Congress finds that:"

☐ The increasing use of computers and sophisticated information technology, while essential to the efficient operations of the Government, has greatly magnified the harm to individual privacy that can occur from any collection, maintenance, use, or dissemination of personal information;

☐ the right of privacy is a personal and fundamental right protected by the Constitution of the United States; and

☐ in order to protect the privacy of individuals identified in information systems maintained by Federal agencies, it is necessary and proper for Congress to regulate the collection, maintenance, use and dissemination of information by such agencies.

The Privacy Act had three major provisions designed to protect personal privacy. First, it allowed an individual's access to his or her federal government file upon request. Second, it required that information going into all files had to be "timely" and "accurate." Third, it required government agencies to make lists of all requests for files and to supply the names of those who had requested personal files concerning the individual involved, upon demand.

Critics are fond of pointing to the Privacy Act's inadequacies. Many files, for example, are excluded from the disclosure requirement. These files cannot be reviewed by the person named in them, even though they may contain damaging and inaccurate information.

But the critics believe the chief reason for the failure of the Privacy Act is that it has no teeth. The Office of Management and Budget (OMB) was charged with overseeing implementation of the act, but OMB does not have the staff necessary to review computer operations throughout the large bureaucracy. Moreover, as critics point out, the Privacy Act permits each federal agency to police itself. Each agency can decide which files it will turn over upon request and which it will exclude from disclosure. This leaves too much highly personal information, the critics conclude, at the disposal of federal bureaucrats.

Major Daniel Fannin, a computer specialist for the Department of Defense, has said that the changes brought by the Privacy Act are "cosmetic" and "superficial." Many government agencies, he claims, have kept record systems that violate the provisions of the act, and continue to do so. Moreover, he adds, government employees are still negligent and careless about the information they control.

The 1974 Family Educational Rights and Privacy Act (FERPA). School records play an important part in almost every person's life. They contain our grades and evaluations of our work and behavior from kindergarten through high school and on, if we attend college and graduate school. But they also contain much more. They contain comments by teachers on our character and ability. They may also contain medical records, psychological, IQ, and personality tests scores, and other such information.

These records will follow a student as he or she moves from one school to another, and will be used to evaluate the student's ability and character by administrators and teachers who may have no personal knowledge of the student. The information lodged in school records also may play a part in being accepted or rejected for college admission or for a job.

Because school records play such an important role in our lives, it would seem important that students or their parents have the right to review their records for contents and accuracy. Before 1974, however, most school records were closed to students and parents alike. If they contained inaccuracies or misstatements, those inaccuracies or misstatements would stand unless spotted by a school administrator—an unlikely event.

Congress opened up school records with the Family Educational Rights and Privacy Act. Among other things, FERPA provided that:

(1) Students over eighteen had the right to see their records, if the school they attended received funds from the U.S. Department of Education. The parents of a student under eighteen could view school records, as long as the student gave his or her permission.

(2) No charge was to be made for reviewing the records, and the student or parents were to be permitted to make copies of the records for their own personal use.

(3) Inaccuracies and misstatements found in the records could be changed. In order to make changes in the records, the student would be permitted a hearing before school authorities. If school authorities denied the need for any change, then the student would be allowed to attach a personal statement to his or her record, explaining any disagreements with the records.

(4) Disclosure of school records to outside parties was severely limited, and school authorities were required to keep a log of all parties requesting a student's records.

(5) If a student believed that his or her rights under FERPA were being disregarded or violated by school officials, then a complaint could be lodged with the HEW.

For the first time, FERPA opened up school records that had been closed to students. Privacy advocates, however, have found shortcomings in the act. First, they note, it does not apply to private schools, only to those that receive grants from the U. S. Department of Education.

Second, one provision of the act makes it possible for school guidance counselors to demand that students sign a statement (before any letters are written) that they will never ask to see letters of recommendation written for them by teachers. This assures that the letters will be frank and to the point, but it also means that the student will never be permitted to clear up misstatements that may exist in the letters.

Third, privacy advocates are concerned that FERPA permits too many disclosures of school records to outside parties, in spite of the act's attempt to limit disclosures. The act, for example, permits disclosure of school records to persons involved in granting financial aid to students, to testing, research, and accrediting organizations, and to other parties.

The problem with any disclosure of personal information to outside sources, the privacy advocates explain, is that the person involved loses control of that information. Private data then becomes available to so large a number of people that any safeguards on privacy are meaningless. In the computer age, they point out, what once had been held in the secrecy of school records, can quickly become accessible to anyone who might want to dig it up.

The Privacy Commission. In 1977, the Privacy Protection Study Commission, a special presidential panel, issued a report that warned that personal privacy was endangered in American society as never before. Entitled "Personal Privacy in an Information Society," the report was an exhaustive 654-page analysis of the privacy issue.

"By opening more avenues for collection of information," the report said, "government has enormously broadened its opportunities both to help and to embarrass, harass, and injure the individual." These dangers, it added, are "real, not mythical." In fact, the report stated, the dangers are so real that they involve "social and political value choices of the most basic kind. . . . As long as America believes . . . in the worth of the individual citizen, it must constantly reaffirm and reinforce its protections for the privacy, and ultimately the autonomy, of the individual."

Noting that "neither law nor technology now gives an individual the tools he needs to protect his legitimate interest in the records organizations keep about him," the panel made numerous recommendations to shore up the right to privacy. Among those recommendations were the following:

☐ That Federal law be enacted or amended to forbid an employer from using the polygraph or other truth-verification equipment to gather information from an applicant or employee.

☐ That an employer articulate, communicate, and implement fair information practice policies for employment records. . . .

☐ That Federal law be enacted or amended to provide that an individual shall have a right to see and copy, upon request, all recorded information concerning him that a credit grantor has used to make an adverse credit decision about him.

☐ That the Privacy Act of 1974 permit the recovery of special and general damages sustained by an individual as a result of a violation of the Act, but in no case should a person entitled to recovery receive less than the sum of $1,000 or more than the sum of $10,000 for general damages in excess of the dollar amount of any special damages.

☐ That the Congress provide by statute that no record or information contained therein collected or maintained for a research of statistical purpose under Federal authority or with Federal funds may be used in individually identifiable form to make any decision or take any action directly affecting the individual to whom the record pertains, except within the context of the research plan or protocol, or with the specific authorization of such individual.

In 1979, two years after the Privacy Commission issued its report, President Jimmy Carter used its recommendations as the basis for a program of "privacy proposals" he sent to Congress for consideration. Since that time, however, Congress has done nothing about the proposals and their fate is uncertain.

The Right of Financial Privacy Act of 1978 (RFPA). In 1970, Congress passed the Bank Secrecy Act, which required all banks to keep complete records of every financial transaction undertaken within the bank. The purpose of the act was to enable the Department of Treasury to identify people who used their bank accounts to disguise illegal transactions or to avoid paying taxes. Under the law, banks were required to microfilm the front and back of every check and keep the microfilm on record for five years.*

Law enforcement officials and others had long made use of banking records to keep track of individuals and identify their activities. The Bank Secrecy Act increased the amount of information available to investigators.

Many Americans regarded the provisions of the banking act as dangerous to privacy. "I don't have to recount for you here," said Congressman Fortney Stark (Democrat, California) before Congress, "what a clear and concise and detailed record...even the most naive financial person could build on anyone of us here if he could take our canceled checks..." and use them to investigate our activities.

The Republican Task Force of the House of Representatives also noticed the danger to personal privacy. Banks, it noted, have "become the compilers and custodians of financial records which, when improperly used, enable an individual's entire life-style to be tracked down."

And the Privacy Commission noticed the problem. "When it costs the bank little or nothing to disclose detailed record information," the commission said, "when there are no legal barriers to such disclosure, and when the

---

*There was a great deal of opposition to this provision and it was altered to require banks to keep records of checks and other transactions of $100 or more. In practice, however, most banks have found it easier to microfilm all checks rather than select only those over $100.

goodwill of those on whom the banker must rely for co-operation or services, such as law enforcement officers, can be increased, the pressures to disclose become enormous and often insurmountable."

Hopes that the Supreme Court might provide prohibitions on the disclosure of bank accounts proved illusory. In the 1976 *United States* v. *Miller* case, the Court declared that "We perceive no legitimate 'expectation of privacy'" in a person's checks or deposit slips, or in microfilm copies of the same items. "The checks are not confidential communications, but negotiable instruments to be used in commercial transactions."

Bank statements, the Court went on, "contain only information voluntarily conveyed to the banks and exposed to their employees in the ordinary course of business." When a depositor uses a bank, it concluded, he or she "takes the risk, in revealing his affairs to another, that the information will be conveyed by that person to the government."

In 1978, with a bill called the Right of Financial Privacy Act, Congress addressed the problem of disclosure of banking statements. The act was designed to limit the federal government's access to private financial information and required government agencies to inform a person before an investigation was made of his or her bank account.

Critics of the act, however, say that the RFPA has had little effect on the problems it was designed to alleviate. There are too many exceptions to the act's provisions, they claim. The CIA, the Secret Service, and other agencies are exempt, and under certain "emergency" situations, any agency may waive the requirement to inform a person that his or her bank account is to be investigated.

Furthermore, the critics point out, the act does not go to the root of the problem. The Bank Secrecy Act of 1970 still stands, and banks are still required to microfilm or record financial transactions. The information is still there for those who might want to use it.

In this chapter we have concentrated on problems of privacy involving government files, school records, and banking transactions. In the computer age, however, all personal data is subject to computerization and any information about ourselves that we turn over to others can become part of a data bank. Medical records, tax reports, and criminal records are all subject to misuse—and to becoming part of a computer's store of information over which we have little or no control.

In earlier chapters, we saw how the right to privacy gradually worked its way into American law. We also saw how the Supreme Court brought Fourth Amendment privacy safeguards to bear on unreasonable searches and seizures and how it expanded those safeguards to include wiretapping and other forms of electronic surveillance.

In regard to computers, however, privacy law is still in its infancy. The Supreme Court has yet to speak on the threats to privacy presented by computers. According to privacy advocates, Congress has yet to address that threat with effective and forceful laws.

In 1973, the Department of Health, Education, and Welfare came up with a code of "fair information practices" regarding computers and privacy. The HEW code served as the basis of the Privacy Act of 1974. Its five clearly stated principles were:

1) There must be no personal-data record-keeping systems whose existence is a secret.

2) There must be a way for an individual to find out what information about him or her is in a record and how it is used.

3) There must be a way for an individual to prevent information about him or her obtained for one purpose from being used or made available for other purposes without consent.

4) There must be a way for an individual to correct or amend a record of identifiable information about him or her.

5) Any organization using records identifiable to a person must ensure the reliability of the data for their intended use and must take reasonable precautions to prevent misuse of the data.

Many privacy advocates have praised these five principles, but believe that much still needs to be done before they will become effective law.

In 1973 and 1974, the International Business Machine Corporation (IBM) conducted a study of its own that developed guidelines similar to HEW's and applied them to its own corporate enterprise. Other large corporations have established comparable programs. Observers debate the effectiveness of these programs, but agree that important first steps have been taken. In addition, ten states have enacted their own codes for fair information practices.

Privacy advocates, however, doubt that the answer to the threat to privacy by computers lies in a voluntary, organization by organization, or state by state, reform of computer practices. Instead, they look to stronger legislation by Congress. "Real protection in this world," said Charles Reich, a former Yale University law professor and a strong privacy advocate, "comes not from people's good intentions, but from the law."

10
CONCLUSION

Perhaps in the long run the fight
to preserve privacy is a vain one.
But, like the struggle to preserve
life, it must be continued while
any shred of privacy remains.
From an August 9, 1966
editorial in *The New York Times*

The right to privacy exists. The Supreme Court has declared that there are certain matters, involving family relationships, that must remain forever outside the sphere of government intrusion. Common law provides a means to take legal action against violations of privacy. In many cases, the courts have protected the individual from violations of constitutional rights, such as the right to remain silent and the right against unreasonable searches and seizures.

The right to privacy, however, is not absolute, nor has it kept up with the development of modern technology. The fabric of law, tradition, and safeguards that protect personal privacy is still too weak to confront the computer society. Even wiretapping, which has been in existence for more than a hundred years, has never been brought under control.

Clearly, if privacy is a right and a value worth preserving—and this author believes that it is—something more needs to be done. The flow of private and confidential information to computers needs to be restricted. The belief that computers necessarily promise a better future needs to be challenged. The faith that our modern civilization has in its machines must be examined.

All this, of course, will take time and as time passes, technology advances and presents us with new problems. Perhaps the most optimistic assessment we can make about the future of privacy is that privacy is now a deep concern of many Americans and the subject of widespread discussion. Out of this concern and discussion may come the laws and safeguards needed to preserve a modicum of personal autonomy, privacy, and freedom of choice in the computer age.

SUGGESTED READING

An asterisk (*) denotes books of interest to younger readers.

Breckenridge, A. C. *The Right to Privacy*. Lincoln, NE: University of Nebraska, 1970. (Traces the development of the right to privacy in American legal history. The appendix reprints in full the 1890 article on the "Right to Privacy" written by Charles Warren and Louis Brandeis.)

*Brenton, Myron. *The Privacy Invaders*. New York: Coward McCann, 1964. (Still useful and interesting today.)

*Ernst, Morris and Alan Schwartz. *The Right to Be Let Alone*. Westport, CT: Greenwood Press, 1962. (A good, overall look at the right to privacy.)

*French, Scott. *The Big Brother Game*. San Francisco, CA: GNU Publishing, 1976. (A "how to" book: how to build wiretaps, bugs, and other electronic devices.)

Garrison, Omar. *Spy Government: the Emerging Police State in America*. Secaucus, N.J.: Lyle Stuart, 1967. (An extreme view of the state of the right to privacy in America.)

*Gillers, Stephen. *Getting Justice: The Rights of People*. New York: New American Library, 1973. (An excellent summary of the civil rights enjoyed by Americans.)

*Hayden, Trudy and Jack Novik. *Your Rights to Privacy*. New York: Avon, 1980. (This helpful book is a publication of the American Civil Liberties Union and is subtitled "The Basic ACLU Guide for Your Rights to Privacy.")

Hoffman, Lance. *Computers and Privacy in the Next Decade*. New York: Academic Press, 1980. (A thoughtful and technical look by computer scientists and experts.)

*Le Mond, Alan and Ron Fry. *No Place to Hide*. New York: Saint Martin's Press, 1975. (A good journalistic account of the threats to privacy.)

*Long, Edward. *The Intruders: The Invasion of Privacy by Government and Industry*. New York: Praeger, 1966. (Perhaps no United States Senator, with the exception of Sam Ervin, has been as concerned with privacy as Senator Long.)

Lykken, David Thoreson. *A Tremor in the Blood. Uses and Abuses of the Lie Detector*. New York: McGraw-Hill, 1980. (A thorough-going and scientific discussion of the lie-detector and its threat to personal privacy.)

*Mayer, Michael. *Rights of Privacy*. New York: Law Arts, 1972. (Good introduction to the subject.)

Miller, Arthur. *The Assault on Privacy: Computers, Data Banks, and Dossiers*. Ann Arbor, MI: University of Michigan Press, 1971. (A first-rate account of the threats to privacy presented by computers. Thorough and well-documented.)

*Packard, Vance. *The Naked Society*. New York: McKay, 1964. (This best-seller, now almost twenty years old, awakened many Americans to the threat to privacy.)

*Petrocelli, William. *Low Profile: How to Avoid the Privacy Invaders*. New York: McGraw-Hill, 1981. (An excellent and very readable account of the state of privacy in the United States today.)

Rosenberg, Jerry. *The Death of Privacy*. New York: Random House, 1969. (A pessimistic statement about privacy rights.)

*Rowan, Ford. *Technospies*. New York: G.P. Putnam's Sons, 1978. (An excellent summary of what technology can do today.)

Rule, James B. *Private Lives and Public Surveillance: Social Control in the Computer Age*. New York: Schocken, 1974. (Excellent on the implications of the computer revolution.)

*Sherick, L. G. *How to Use the Freedom of Information Act*. New York: Arco, 1978. (Excellent summary of the history behind the Freedom of Information Act and of the privileges it grants Americans.)

*Smith, Robert Ellis. *Privacy: How to Protect What's Left of It*. New York: Doubleday, 1980. (Excellent and very readable summary of the threat to privacy in modern America. A lawyer and privacy advocate, Smith has been called the "Ralph Nader of privacy." He is also editor of the nation's foremost journal on privacy problems, the Washington, D.C.-based *Privacy Journal*.)

Westin, Alan. *Privacy and Freedom*. New York: Atheneum, 1967. (Westin published this book as Director of the Center for Research and Education in American Liberties at Columbia University. He is one of the foremost experts on privacy in America today.)

*Wicklein, John. *Electronic Nightmare: the New Communications and Freedom*. New York: Viking, 1981. (A very interesting and readable summary of modern technology and its effect on privacy.)

The following four publications contain information gathered during government sponsored investigations of threats to privacy:

*Hearings Before the Subcommittee of the Committee on Government Operations, House of Representatives. *The Computer and Invasion of Privacy* (1967).

*Public Affairs Press. *Uncle Sam is Watching You: Highlights from the Hearings of the Senate Subcommittee on Constitutional Rights* (1971).

*Report of the Secretary's Advisory Committee on Automated Personnel Data Systems, U.S. Department of Health, Education, & Welfare. *Records, Computers, and the Rights of Citizens* (1973).

The Report of the Privacy Protection Study Commission. *Personal Privacy in an Information Society* (1977).

INDEX

Abortion, 29, 37–41
American Civil Liberties
  Union, 116
Assault on Privacy, The
  (Miller), 123–126
Assembly, freedom of, 17,
  35
Association, right of, 35
Autonomy, 122

Bank Secrecy Act of 1970,
  133–134
Banking records, 133–134
Barthel, Joan, 112
Bayh, Birch, 115, 116
Beany, William, 81
Black, Hugo, 36, 37, 41, 65
Blackmun, Harry, 37–39,
  62
Blacks, 20
Blackstone, Sir William, 29
Blews, Don, 113
Blue-streak monitoring, 72
Boyd v. *United States*
  (1886), 47, 51, 52
Bradley, Joseph, 47–48
Brandeis, Louis, 6, 15,
  21–25, 79–81
Brave New World (Huxley),
  10, 12
Brennan, William, 65,
  90–91
Bugging, 71, 75–76

Burton, Harold, 89
Butler, Pierce, 79

Camara v. *Municipal Court
  of the City and County of
  San Francisco* (1967),
  62, 63
Carter, Jimmy, 132
Central Intelligence
  Agency (CIA), 101
Chimel v. *California* (1969),
  59–60
Clark, Tom, 50
Cobb, Judge, 31
Common law, 21–24,
  29–33, 139
Computers, 6, 13, 121–136
Constitution of the United
  States, 17–20
Contraception, 29, 33–37
Cooley, Thomas M., 6*n*,
  18–19, 22
Coolidge, Calvin, 77
Corporations, 5
Craven, J. Braxton, Jr.,
  27
Credit, 5, 121, 126–128

Dash, Samuel, 90
Death in Canaan (Barthel),
  112
Declaration of
  Independence, 17